Leadership Lessons from a Team Captain

LEADERSHIP
LESSONS
from a
TEAM CAPTAIN

The Guide to Leading Teams
with Trust, Transparency and Empathy

CIARA UNGAR

NEW YORK

LONDON • NASHVILLE • MELBOURNE • VANCOUVER

Leadership Lessons from a Team Captain

The Guide to Leading Teams with Trust, Transparency and Empathy

Published in New York, New York, by Morgan James Publishing. Morgan James is a trademark of Morgan James, LLC. www.MorganJamesPublishing.com

Proudly distributed by Ingram Publisher Services.

Project coordination by Ciara Ungar at CiaraUngar.com

Morgan James BOGO™

A **FREE** ebook edition is available for you or a friend with the purchase of this print book.

CLEARLY SIGN YOUR NAME ABOVE

Instructions to claim your free ebook edition:
1. Visit MorganJamesBOGO.com
2. Sign your name CLEARLY in the space above
3. Complete the form and submit a photo of this entire page
4. You or your friend can download the ebook to your preferred device

ISBN 9781631956638 paperback
ISBN 9781631956645 ebook
Library of Congress Control Number:
2021939739

Cover Design by:
Megan Dillon
megan@creativeninjadesigns.com

Interior Design by:
Christopher Kirk
www.GFSstudio.com

Portrait Photography:
Jordan E. Andre Photography

Morgan James is a proud partner of Habitat for Humanity Peninsula and Greater Williamsburg. Partners in building since 2006.

Get involved today! Visit MorganJamesPublishing.com/giving-back

I'd like to thank some of the most profound educators I had the pleasure of learning from: K. Moore, J. Bay, C. Croxford. Thank you for pushing me to be my best and providing a strong foundation for pursuing my dreams of becoming an author. The release of this book puts me officially on this path and I owe that possibility to you.

I'd also like to thank my former and current teammates and coaches. Without you, I would not have learned about leadership and teamwork. To one of the most impactful coaches in my life, M. Thompson, may you rest in peace knowing you were loved and a part of my success story.

Finally, to one of the greatest leaders I have had the chance to learn from to this day, B. Jackson, thank you for teaching me that being human first creates greater success as a leader than any other quality. I have carried your laughter, friendship and example with me through-out my career and will forever be imprinted with your wisdom.

CONTENTS

A team is not a group of people who work together.
A team is a group of people who trust each other.
@simonsinek

INTRODUCTION

Today's workforce is a clashing of generations. Traditional business models are on the cusp of transitioning into more modern ways of working and the increase in knowledge work is shifting the demands of our teams. There is also a clashing of values as we are at a unique time in history when there is the greatest number of coexisting generations and value systems. There is no better testament to this reality than when COVID-19 hit in early 2020 and the world nearly shut down in its entirety and we saw cultural differences rise to the forefront of discussions. Businesses with more traditional models that fought to resist the transition to remote work, virtual meetings, and contactless sales pitches were suddenly forced to evaluate their viability in this new reality—one that many expected to happen eventually in the next decade, just not suddenly within a few weeks. Many of these businesses didn't survive the quick transition because they ignored the shift and hadn't set a foundation that prepared its business for what would come, leading to an estimated 47M+ US job losses during Q1-Q2 in a single fiscal year.

If you're reading this book, the chances you were affected by this devastating shift in the economy are high. If you are one of the lucky ones who was not affected, without a doubt, you know someone who was. This impact on the economy is historical—not just in the US, but across the world—and will take years to recover from. But, I'm not here to discuss business viability in preparation for the next pandemic or global shutdown. I am here to talk about one of the most important lessons that came out of this worldwide event, one that many businesses overlooked and consequently weren't able to sustain a very difficult and very challenging season because of: leadership.

The topic of leadership has weighed heavily on my conscience and heart for many years. I remember what it was like to be a grossly ineffective leader early in my career when I was inexperienced and narrow-minded. It took a few personal and professional battles to open my eyes to what was working well and what was tarnishing professional relationships and stunting team growth. The better part of the last decade has been focused on working through life-altering health issues and life transitions well before COVID-19 struck the world overnight. These major life events taught me a lot about myself, my strengths and weaknesses, and my leadership (for better or for worse), and I've been eagerly awaiting the right time to extend what I've learned to others. The global pandemic was the push I needed. Not only was it the first real opportunity I had to devote time to developing my thoughts, but it was also an experience almost every other American could relate to and unfortunately felt the effects of. Although the pandemic brought about a lot of tragedy for millions of people, it also brought about a lot of fruitful learning opportunities. Many business leaders did not take the opportunity to reflect on their own habits and ways of conducting business when their businesses struggled, even when the media and employee complaints were against them. Businesses were greatly affected by the pandemic alongside equal rights movements, and without a proper foundation or strong leadership, they faltered. Not all, but many.

Like many of my peers, I was put on furlough early in the pandemic, which led to seven months of unemployment and eventual layoff. The furlough announcement for my team and colleagues came as a surprise— two days prior, our executive staff ensured our teams wouldn't be making cuts and were in a great financial position to last months ahead. For many people in my company, our experience went something like this:

- March 20, Friday Afternoon: Company-wide meeting announcing we were in a stable financial position for the foreseeable future months out and no one should worry about losing their jobs.
- March 24, Tuesday Late Evening: Received an all-hands virtual meeting invite for Wednesday, 9:30 AM.
- March 25, Wednesday, 9:30 AM: Executive team signs on to virtual meeting and reads from a script to let all staff know they would be laying off members of the company. If you were part of this group, you would receive a meeting invite for one of three meetings in the following two hours and would be paid for their work up to that day but not beyond.

- March 25, Wednesday 9:50 AM - 11:30 AM: Staff anxiously awaited to see if they were selected to receive a meeting invite 10 minutes before their slaying call. When calls were conducted, it was scripted with little explanation as to the sudden change from just a few days prior and little—if any—empathy for its impact. On this call, I recall one executive team member noting how they were taking pay cuts (which still left them at nearly seven figures) and felt the pain of this as if to empathize, while those they were speaking to were losing their livelihood.

I liken this experience to a mass slaying because that's how it was organized and how it felt being on the receiving end. Overnight, leadership had gone from communicating to its staff who worked tirelessly and thanklessly to sustain the company's growth they were safe for a long time to within just a few days they wouldn't be paid past that day and were without a job— and done so in one of the most agonizing ways I could probably think of. Now, I don't include this reflection here as a rant or as an attempt at slander. I include this here as an example that many can relate to in the year 2020 and to demonstrate the impact of leadership that fails its teams in the most important moments. Something I'll revisit later in this book.

*****

I feel it is important to pause here to look through an objective lens. The 2020 global pandemic struck the nation and the world quickly and without remorse. It forced companies to take measures they weren't prepared to handle, and it was nearly impossible to predict what would happen and how a business should prepare. Many companies had to act overnight to transition to remote work and the business models for a lot of companies simply weren't set up for this. My company was one of those, so I must express my utmost respect for leadership teams worldwide that had to work through tough analyses and decisions with little precedent to guide. Like many, I do believe choices had to be made to sustain the business's existence. As someone who has led teams before, I understand the difficulty of affecting one's livelihood and the weight this can bear.

However, my personal experience during the pandemic highlighted several pitfalls of leadership when it mattered most. I share this experience not to slander the company or those involved in the decision-making process, but because I believe we're all susceptible to mistakes (I'll cover many of my own through this book) and believe that the COVID-19 experience created many situations like this across industries that demonstrated the true values and foundations of companies. Situations like this that happened across industries showed us how important humans *should* be in the decision-making process of businesses and how leaders can do better at being human.

*****

Many companies forced into similar situations overnight maintained their staff loyalty and respect by the way they handled tough decisions. I believe without a doubt that employee retention comes from considering teams as more than a means to an end and it shouldn't take a global pandemic to highlight for executive teams where they fall short. But here we are, with an opportunity to learn. Most professionals who were placed on furlough or laid off during COVID-19—whether at my company or not—understood the unprecedented circumstances and more or less anticipated it happening at some point, as angering and scary as it was. Many companies took the right steps to ensure empathy was shown (not just spoken of) and those companies are the ones that retained their respect and potential sustained growth. But many companies did not, and the mishandling only worked against them in recovery.

Some errors that could have avoided backlash and retained employee trust and respect in my own circumstance:

- **Transparency.** It's likely I'll never know what discussions were happening in the background. As an employee, I only know that my employer told me one thing and executed another. Although it's beneficial in some ways to avoid panic, being transparent and honest about the plausibility of near-future layoffs would have created trust.
- **Pre-Announcement of Layoff Calls.** If the goal was to avoid panic for the 24 hours leading up, it was counteracted by the panic caused that morning. Not only did employees feel blindsided, but they were also thrust into panic and forced to wait with the worst-case scenario replaying in their minds. This is the opposite display of empathy.
- **Scripted Calls.** This was one of the more difficult parts of the experience. The mass layoff calls had little infor-

mation and were a scripted four-minute read-out that included insensitive commentary around the layoffs and pay cuts.

- **Generic Follow-Ups.** In a day when many lost their livelihood, generic email follow-ups with no display of empathy were sent following the layoff calls.
- **Poor Communication.** Overall, a lack of communication included empathy and clear information, which made a terrible situation worse to work through.

In this circumstance, it would have been a nightmare for the executive team and/or Human Resources to have made individual calls to each person placed on furlough or laid off. I can sympathize with this challenge. But this nightmare was nothing compared to those facing losing health care during a global pandemic, suddenly losing income with no severance offered (for furlough), etc. Despite how challenging it would have been, the empathetic and human approach would have been to make those calls individually. Many noteworthy companies in several industries did make these calls individually, which earned positive press coverage and the utmost respect of their employees.

Again, I share this experience – not to slander, but – to set the relatable foundation of the through-line that serves as a cornerstone of this entire book. The companies that took the empathetic approach during the COVID-19 global pandemic are the companies that I believe will sustain any economic shift they may face long-term. An empathetic approach to leadership is not always the easiest – in fact, it rarely is the easiest approach and is not one that comes naturally for most. Often, this has to be trained and engrained. But it *is* possible to serve the businesses' best interest while also upholding an empathetic leadership style, which ultimately will support the sustainability of your growth as a company and enable you to weather any storm. It comes down to the willingness to go that extra mile because you care to and are equipped to mentally/emotionally.

With this in mind, the goal of this book is to outline characteristics and behaviors of leadership I believe apply to leaders at any level and in any industry. I draw on my and others' experience as an athlete, and my personal hurdles in the last decade, which have forced me to adopt a new understanding of what leadership looks like and where many get it wrong, including myself. It's my hope that the next generation of business owners and team leads can build more sustainable business models by treating those who make their business run as more than a means to an end. To do this, it starts with leadership, at the top all the way to the bottom.

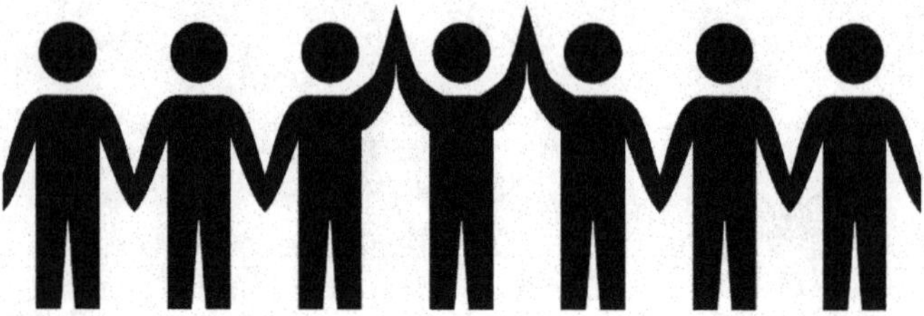

PART 1
FOUNDATIONS

1

PSYCHOLOGY OF LEADERSHIP

drivers of decision-making, motivation and influence

L eadership, good or bad, can have a profound impact on whether a team succeeds or fails. A poor leader can take a company down quickly, just as a good leader can drive his or her team to excel quickly. And, although business smarts can take you far, it's emotional intelligence that helps you cross the finish line. There are varying opinions on what constitutes a "good leader" vs a "poor leader," and different definitions of success, but what remains consistent is the notion that leadership is important and reflective of whether a team will succeed. A leader has the unique role of both setting the vision for the path toward growth and also creating motivation within the environment and their teams to achieve that growth. Good leadership itself is one of the greatest competitive advantages a business can have, but there's more to *why* than what meets the eye. The advantages of leadership go beyond decision-making capabilities and extend into multiple dimensions rooted in the psychology of the human brain and what drives people to perform their best.

Team member motivators fall within one of two categories: they are rational or irrational. Rational motivations are conscious and include gaining money, status, *FOMO* (fear of missing out) and power. Although these are universal truths (we need money to eat, have a roof over our head, and survive), how much they are most influential varies from person to person. As leaders, these are a bit easier for us to control, because we can give raises, promotions, and titles. Our second type of motivation, the irrational motivators, are usually more influential to us as individuals. These motivators go beyond our ability as leaders to control because they're deeply rooted in one's unconscious and include impactful images, experiences, and emotions that can be projected onto the relationships we have with others, including our leaders. It's these irrational motivators we live and breathe each moment and that influence who we are as people—and professionals. Unfortunately, these motivators are harder to define and recognize as leaders.

In most professions, there are seasons of stress and periods of calm. The times of calm consists of us sitting at our desks, answering emails or phone calls, and having a workload we can manage without significant stretch required. Overall, these are unremarkable days, but many would say for every one calm day we have, there are four days that are hectic and stressful. Calm isn't the norm for most and stress happens, whether it's a deadline you're trying to meet, a question you don't know the answer to, an escalated problem to solve, or a new skill to learn. These seasons of organizational stress *are* the norm, and it is in these situations we become more influenced by our irrational motivators—we need encouragement, praise and protection (a phenomenon of paternal and maternal transference explored by Freud), just as one needs from their trusted parental figures who have guided them through life. People, in a subconscious way, put their leaders in the position of fulfilling these parental attributes, looking for encouragement, praise and protection from their managers and higher leadership. Without that stamp of approval, teams ultimately become demotivated through tensions, disassociation, and distrust.

SOCIAL INFLUENCE

Social influence is also at play when observing the psychology of leadership and teams. An added layer of rational and irrational motivators falls around social influence, the process wherein "one person's attitudes, cognitions, or behaviors are changed through the doings of another"[1] and as the "myriad of ways that people impact one another, including change in attitudes, beliefs, feelings and behavior, that results from the comments, actions, or even the mere presence of others."[2] In other words, we modify our behaviors based on the presence or actions of others. There are four primary forms of social influence we experience daily: Under *conformity*, we change our beliefs and behaviors; through *compliance*, we temporarily change our behavior to agree publicly, but privately disagree and do not believe in the behavior; *internalization* occurs when we agree publicly and privately and adopt the viewpoint and behavior of a group; and lastly, *identification* extends across several areas of external behavior when someone conforms to demands or expectations of their social role in society, but their internal opinion or values do not change.

These forms of influence can be at play within a team dynamic, but they all maintain a common truth: we take cues from those around us that tell us how to feel, think and act. In today's environment, we most easily understand and think of social influence as the brand ambassadors giving us discount codes on Instagram (influencers), but the phenomenon also holds true within team dynamics in the workplace. We let the pressures and expectations of others shape our behaviors and decisions.

Sometimes, social influence impacts our ability to fit in. It is in our DNA to want to conform to and fit in with those around us, so this is a particularly strong force within social influence. We make decisions at work we feel will be uncontested and popular to avoid being difficult, viewed as challenging to work with or delaying progress. Team members may mimic the behavior of their leader or decide they believe what their leader would agree with simply to fit in. In other cases, standing out is also a force at play within the social influence. Even a team unit has its own unique team members who all are differentiated—even if they publicly make decisions that others want them to make. Identity is another force in the workplace within the realm of social influence as employees want to identify with a brand or product they align with.

But, perhaps of most impact on leadership is the ability of social influence to drive productivity and performance. Here, as leaders, we can design effective working environments, shape situations and outcomes, and build teams that bolster high performance. People work harder when others are around. We want others to see that we, too, are putting in the time, are part of the team and contributing to the goal—a form of seeking both to be praised and to fit in. Social comparison and competition are motivators for team members to work harder, but only when the comparison to their peers is within proximity and the gap is fairly narrow.

CULTURAL & GENERATIONAL GAPS

Motivations and social influence aside, there is yet another element at play that impacts the dynamic of leadership. Gaps in generations (and even cultural differences) have a profound impact on much of today's workforce with leadership. Depending on one's generation, organizational structure and leadership look different, paths to success look different, and even defining what success is looks different. All that is to say that each generation has its own value system, which plays an important role in team dynamics. In our quest to understand leadership, collaboration and team dynamics, we have to look no further than outside the workplace (or the team) itself and at our own experiences. You have likely had a coworker or two that you've noticed is a completely different person at home or with friends than they are Monday through Friday in the office or on Zoom. We *could* easily point to one primary cause for this: an office environment bringing out a certain side of a person that is a direct reflection of the culture and socialization they've been exposed to outside of that workplace. If we are to understand—and I mean truly understand—why people act and behave the way they do to become better leaders for them, we have to start there: cultural and social influences on people and how that translates into who they are in the workplace. One of the biggest tensions in today's workforce (and culture at large) is rooted in generational differences, so I'd like to start our focus there.

Traditional vs New Age Expectations

Differences in how people have grown accustomed to work environments have a profound impact on how they interact within them and what they expect from others in them. Traditional work environments are more concrete with nine-to-five work hours, fixed long-term teams, labor-based skills and bureaucratic operations, which can create structure, stability and a central authority with a clear chain of command. Personal challenges and interests of the employees of traditional environments are virtually non-existent, and what happens outside of work stays outside of work and should not affect your performance. In many ways, we can look at the traditional work environment as conservative yet predictable. This work environment creates consistency, but it also creates a level of professionalism and order that spills over into communication styles and work-life balance. It also fosters a separation of the human aspect of the workplace. The psychological impact of traditional work environments is a give-and-take of feeling comfortable and knowing what you can expect and rely on, but it is not a place that has room for the weight you bear outside of its walls.

In contrast, the new-age office creates drastically different environments and expectations and centers on knowledge work, as coined by Maura Nevel Thomas in *Work Without Walls*. Culturally, the new-age workplace encourages self-help and acceptance, work-life balance, interdependence, agility, and empowerment. There's a sense of requirement that one be passionate about what they do. A four-year degree isn't always required and a willingness to fail and try new ways of operating are encouraged. Flexibility is valued and designed into the workday to reduce stress and generate fulfillment. Beyond culture, we can see that the modern workplace is inundated with technologies that keep work environments deeply connected (even distracted), so much so that there's an invasion of personal life and work-life becomes embedded. The need for formalities is unnecessary and individuality is not only celebrated but is also rooted in who the company becomes as a public identity. The modern work environment creates a sense of connection, a blended reality, heightening vulnerabilities and a further strengthening of internal motivators. And, because there are unknowns and a constant evolution of policy, operations and opportunity, there is an interesting psychological dynamic of the modern work environment. Flexibility and pivoting quickly are highly valued, so there's little room for staying stagnant or holding too tight to the "rules." Perhaps one of the most notable differences in the modern work environment is the requirement it has of leadership to—more than ever—be self-aware and possess a high level of emotional intelligence to account for emotional and physical needs of their teams.

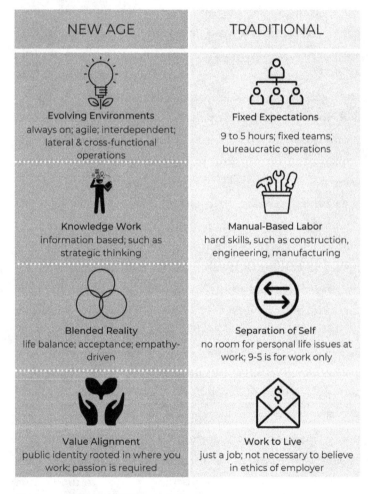

NEW AGE	TRADITIONAL
Evolving Environments always on; agile; interdependent; lateral & cross-functional operations	**Fixed Expectations** 9 to 5 hours; fixed teams; bureaucratic operations
Knowledge Work information based; such as strategic thinking	**Manual-Based Labor** hard skills, such as construction, engineering, manufacturing
Blended Reality life balance; acceptance; empathy-driven	**Separation of Self** no room for personal life issues at work; 9-5 is for work only
Value Alignment public identity rooted in where you work; passion is required	**Work to Live** just a job; not necessary to believe in ethics of employer

Boomer vs Millennial

We understand there is a division between traditional and new-age work environments, but this doesn't just happen because a business started a certain year and randomly operates this way.

Inherent influences create these environments, a lot of which concerns how different generations were raised and the unique challenges and experiences they faced. Between the years of 1880 and 2030, there will be eight generations and we are living in a unique time in history when six of those eight generations are coexisting – in culture and in the workplace – which creates major differences presenting themselves in expectations, operations, values and beyond. Generational differences (mostly between Boomers and Millennials) is one of the, if not *the*, greatest impacts on workplace models today, the use of technologies and need for consistencies being the most obvious presentations. Another example of this impact was highlighted in Lindsay E. Ballinger's 2018 article, *Understanding Socialization Efficacy and Loneliness of Baby Boomers through Facebook*, which highlights the relationship of social media and health, particularly as it pertains to the mental well-being of Boomers.[3] Ballinger shows how research supports that the Boomer generation does and will experience a high-level of chronic disability and long-term care needs, and both environmental and social forces are to blame. What this report inadvertently drives home for my purposes is that the Boomer group is more of a loner group, socially speaking. This generation is highly selective for building friendships and relationships, so earning their trust in the workplace will take time. Boomers experienced financial hardships and cultural shifts in a way that created instability, so they are most attracted to what they can predict and rely on, including teams that don't change and have predictable days. Millennials crave connection and go to great lengths to create that connection with the belief that creating deeper connection creates a better world—learning from one another in different environments and collaborating. They take to social media to express themselves and value authenticity, both giving and receiving it. But perhaps where we really see a generational gap in the workplace is in Millennials' willingness to fail. As a group, they're not afraid to fail, always seek innovation and change and question authority and process to improve—no doubt a side effect of being confident, ambitious and achievement-oriented.

I could go on ad nauseam about the differences in human behavior across generations because I believe it so fundamentally affects every part of our waking life: politics, policies, health, professional career and even household structure. When we look at the generational differences between Boomers and Millennials (and there are many more than covered here in this book) and the cultural differences of traditional and new-age business, we can see how tension is easily created within work environments. It's something we learn as leaders, if not from personal experience, then from trainings, conferences and articles. There are many books, articles and Instagram accounts that explore those topics in great detail. I highlight it here, though, because how we as leaders orchestrate our teams is deeply rooted in understanding the psychology that shapes them. Getting to know your team and its construct and understanding the underlying challenges you're facing embedded within one's cultural and social norms can make a world of difference in your ability to lead those team members. In this book, we'll explore many ways to effectively lead your teams, but it starts with understanding the differences among your teammates you likely cannot change, but rather learn to create harmony with.

Tweetable Takeaways

Let's get social! Being able to share your growth along the way is key to transparency as a leader and building other leaders as you go. Here are important takeaways from this chapter that you can easily share on social using #LeadershipFromATeamCaptain and my handle @CiaraUngar.

- A poor leader can take a company down quickly, just as a good leader can drive their team to excel quickly.

- A leader has the unique role of both setting the vision for the path toward growth and also creating motivation within the environment and its people so growth or success can be achieved.

- Team member motivators are either rational or irrational: Rational motivations are conscious and include gaining money, status, *FOMO* and power. Irrational motivators are significantly more influential to us and are deeply rooted in one's unconscious. They include impactful images, experiences, and emotions that can be projected onto the relationships we have with others, including our leaders.

- There are four primary forms of social influence that we experience on a daily basis: *conformity*, *compliance*, *internalization* and *identification*.

- Due to social influence, we make decisions at work that we feel will be uncontested and popular to avoid being difficult, viewed as challenging to work with or delaying progress. We mimic behavior of our leader or make decisions we believe our leader would agree with simply to fit in.

- 🐦 Social influence has the ability to drive productivity and performance through effective working environments, shape situations and outcomes, and build teams that bolster high performance.

- 🐦 Differences in how people have grown accustomed to work environments has a profound impact on how they interact within them and what they expect from others in them.

- 🐦 The psychological impact of traditional work environments is a give-and-take of feeling comfortable and knowing what you can expect and rely on, but it is not a place that has room for the weight you bear outside of its walls.

- 🐦 Culturally, the modern workplace encourages self-help and acceptance, work-life balance, freedom, and empowerment.

- 🐦 The modern work environment truly creates a sense of connection, heightening vulnerabilities and further strengthening internal motivators.

- 🐦 A difference in the modern work environment from traditional is the requirement it has of leadership to be self-aware and possess a high level of emotional intelligence to be able to account for emotional and physical needs of their teams.

- 🐦 The greatest divide in generations exists between Boomers and Millennials due to the different life experiences they've endured.

2

DEFINING A
TEAM CAPTAIN

leaders are more than their titles,
it's who they are

As the title of this book and introduction allude to, much of the basis of the leadership foundations discussed in this book are derived from my experience as an athlete, both learning from team captains and being one. As an athlete, I took for granted what I was internalizing not realizing that the skills and methods I was learning would carry me through my professional career in ways I wouldn't expect. Perseverance, teamwork, and practice have all made their way into my daily workload and I can't help but think I wouldn't have those skills if I hadn't grown up an athlete. What I learned *as* a team captain and *from* great team captains, however, surpasses all of those skills combined and has translated into my commitment to and continued passion for leadership.

Whether you've played a sport or not, most have heard the term and have a basic understanding of what it means. You probably think of a *team captain* to be a member(s) of the team who makes the decisions, gives the motivational speeches, and so forth. This is certainly a great start, but there is a lot more to this role than those moments of climax—it's a manifestation and way of conducting yourself daily. A team captain accepts that extra level of responsibility, whether it's asked for or not. That responsibility doesn't mean workload, but it certainly means effort or emotional care taken in various capacities. The Association for Sports Psychology provides us with one of the best definitions of a team captain I have found to-date:

> **ASSOCIATION FOR APPLIED SPORTS PSYCHOLOGY**
>
> " "
>
> The position of captain is given to those athletes whom the rest of the team respect and trust to lead the team in the right direction. However, with this great honor also comes great responsibility. A captain must be accountable after a bad performance or practice. Captains are expected to perform in the clutch and lead the team to victory. It is also expected that captains will maintain control in the most pressurized situations and be the model of excellence for their teammates.
>
> @CIARAUNGAR

4

Now, doesn't that sound like what we expect of our team leaders in the business setting? If you weren't yet convinced that sports had relevance to business leadership, it's my hope that the definition here can give you a little nudge. In sports, a team captain is considered a team leader, but we often forget that a team leader in the business setting is also a team captain. As I said previously, being a team captain is more than wearing the colored armband or stitching a "C" on your jersey, just like being a team leader is more than having a "VP" or Manager extension attached to your job title—it's a way of carrying yourself every day in all you do, but also in all you think and feel. A team captain and leader are comprised of certain characteristics, has a team player mentality and is someone others look up to. This means you don't have to have the manager title attached to your role description to be a team captain or leader (we see rising leaders all the time on junior teams). A team leader, above anything else, is one who sets the tone and (ideally) a *good* example for the rest of the team to show up and do their best. For better or for worse, a good team leader will have teammates that mimic their behavior, which brings a lot of opportunity to our doorsteps, but also a lot of responsibility.

Being the team leader is arguably a great honor we become calloused to in the mundane 9-5 workforce, and we can easily see it as an obligation that earns us a higher salary rather than an opportunity to impact the people around us. (This is a mistaken viewpoint and a miss that often leads to business decisions that treat individuals as a means to an end.) The opportunity, when seized, requires certain characteristics, behaviors and mindfulness. In their article, Lauer and Blue[5] outline three characteristics, The Three C's, that define a team captain, which puts us in the right mindset for the remainder of this book.

Caring

If your personal experience during COVID-19 (or other time in your career) nor my story in the introduction wasn't enough for you to take my word for it, perhaps the words of these two gentlemen will convince you. *Caring* is the number one characteristic of a team captain that sets them apart as a leader. This goes beyond just caring for the members of the team itself and extends to their care and passion for the work they do. The leader is responsible for the well-being of its team members, including upholding respect for those team members and doing their part to put an end to behaviors that destroy team chemistry. They are equally responsible for ensuring that they lead by example in the care given to and passion maintained for their output.

How does this translate to real life scenarios in the work place?

Consider the office teams you've been on when a leader doesn't address negative behaviors, or worse, perpetuates them. Reflect for a moment on the times you felt disrespected, misunderstood, or unappreciated by others on your team or even the team leader themselves. Did you stay at that company? Or are you still at that company, but experience a toxic daily weight that discourages you from wanting to perform to the best of your ability? If you stayed, do you feel secure in your job and surroundings? If not, notice how that affects your motivation and ability to focus.

Caring is important because it spills over into the team members doing the work of keeping you in business or making you look good as a manager. Stopping destructive behaviors that kill morale, showing appreciation, and doing both to encourage passion will foster team chemistry and a desire to show up each day willing to give one's best effort (something we'll discuss later in greater detail). This is not something that can be faked while having a true positive impact, but building genuine care - that comes from emotional intelligence and mindfulness - for your work and teams will.

Courageous

Courage is the second of the C's outlined by Lauer and Blue that often is misinterpreted when translating into the business world. Being a courageous team captain, to them, means having the integrity to walk the talk and willingness to step up to the task at hand. "Your actions must embody the core values of the team, especially during times of adversity,"[6] they say.

> *Our actions must embody the core values of the team, especially during times of adversity. Be a model of courage and dedication to your teammates by setting lofty goals and working hard to reach them.*

This means setting aggressive goals and being willing to hold team members, including yourself, accountable for achieving those goals. This makes sense for the business world, too, right? Unfortunately, where I see a lot of leaders get this wrong is the "for better or *for worse*" part of it. Too often, team leaders will accept praise when teams do well (or not share that praise with others) but do not to take responsibility when their team fails to meet goals. It takes less *courage* to redirect blame onto others for "failure" than it does to put ourselves on equal footing at the risk of losing our merit. So, have the courage to include yourself in the value chain of successes and failures, and lead your teams out of failure by allowing those failures to make them stronger as a team. You'll find that when you exhibit this form of courage, it takes vulnerability, a characteristic we'll discuss later in this book.

Consistent

Our last "C" of a team captain as outlined by Lauer and Blue is that of consistency. To illustrate the concept of consistency, I want to pause and allow you to reflect on both personal and professional relationships you have had wherein trust does and does not exist. Think of some relationships on both sides of the spectrum. Why do you trust those individuals? Conversely, why do you not? At first, you might answer you simply know they have your best interest at heart. Perhaps they often tell you the truth even when it's not ideal news for you to hear, so you know you can trust their honesty. But I challenge you to dig a little deeper and try to identify the root of why this foundation of trust exists.

If the subtitle here didn't give it away: we trust because of consistency. But, what does consistency mean or look like? A consistent team captain is not only consistent with their character from person to person but is also consistent through all circumstances and in their commitment even when others are not knowingly watching. *Consistency* is a critical trait for managers looking to build trust—when team members see a difference in treatment from person to person or situation to situation, it can erode trust between you and among them. Captains are a model of consistency, or more accurately put, authenticity. They lead by actions rather than words and maintain who they are and what they believe regardless of the circumstances. Research over time proves that what leaders *do* is far more important than what they *say*. Consistency included.

> **The more that managers uphold their promises and commitments, the more trust your employees will have in you.**

Revisiting our question at the beginning of this segment, consistency not only builds a sense of reliability but also helps build trust with your teammates. With consistency, your teams will know that regardless of whether they like what you say, they can trust you to be honest, which is an invaluable trait that will serve your productivity and long-term success.

To drive this home, I'll offer an anecdote.

The Epitome of Consistency
Drew Brees

Drew Brees and I are both Purdue Alumni, so I have a slight affinity toward him. My personal fangirl aside, Drew Brees—MVP, Super Bowl Champion, record-breaker, award winner, Sports Illustrated Person of the Year (and the list goes on)—is one of the most respected quarterbacks in the NFL. He not only has incredible athleticism and talent, but his leadership style is highly regarded by coaches, teammates and fans alike. When we think of the attributes of a team captain, Brees climbs to the top of the list of the definition. But why? Is it just because he simply shows up to every practice, and that's a form of consistency? Is it because he plays with the same level of enthusiasm and grit nearly every game and practice, and *that* is consistency? Sure, those are forms of consistency and certainly imperative to leading a team. But his consistency is more fundamental than that.

Consistency as a leader must be about who you are every day during trials and wins, on and off the field, and that's what Drew Brees shows us. He leads his teams with his arm and motivation on the field, but he also lives his mantra: "The truth is, you don't learn much from winning, but losing can make you a lot stronger."[7] Brees consistently comes ready to take risks to grow and learn from both the wins and the losses and carries himself with grace through both. One of the most renowned moments in NFL history put Brees in the spotlight for his leadership when he broke the record for NFL single season passing yards with the New Orleans Saints. At a moment when he should have enjoyed being in the spotlight, Brees focused the celebration and cameras on every one of his teammates, coaches, ball boys, equipment managers, trainers and sideline staffers and even a former Saints player who was diagnosed with ALS, who he embraced on the sideline. In this moment, he took the time to let each team member know how important they were to his success. And, those who know him attested that it wasn't just for show...that's genuinely who he is on and off the field.

Brees' character is consistent from what we see *on* the field to what we see *off* the field. Throughout his career, we see Brees giving back to his community and bettering the world around him. Most notably, when he moved to New Orleans, he helped in the effort to repair what had been destroyed after Hurricane Katrina had ripped through causing more than an estimated $150 billion in economic damage.[8] A lot of celebrities rallied to support the area through this devastation, but what makes Drew Brees standout is that he manifests great compassion, and he seeks to be of service to others and give comfort to those in need. He professes to want to be more than a shoulder to cry on—although he frequently offers to be one—, but he walks his talk and lives his life's mission to develop the tools that allow him to be helpful to others beyond just a sympathetic ear.

Drew isn't always a saint, however. He is human as all leaders are, and he is no stranger to making big mistakes. Throughout his career, there has been a bad game or two, bad plays, bad throws, bad losses; there have also been bad days because of bad judgment. Most notably, Drew Brees made headlines in 2020 for his comments regarding kneeling during the national anthem, as Colin Kaepernick did in 2016, when Black Lives Matter protests were gaining attention and misrepresentation in the media. Brees quickly came under fire for his comments with the recognition that although people didn't believe this came from a malin-tended place, it was tone-deaf and harmful to progres-sion toward equality in our country. After teammates, fans and others in the league responded publicly (and privately) to his comments, Brees saw this as a learn-ing moment. He did not defend his actions and instead owned up to them, declaring it a time for him to stop talking and start listening:

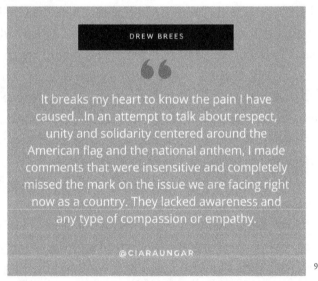

DREW BREES

It breaks my heart to know the pain I have caused...In an attempt to talk about respect, unity and solidarity centered around the American flag and the national anthem, I made comments that were insensitive and completely missed the mark on the issue we are facing right now as a country. They lacked awareness and any type of compassion or empathy.

@CIARAUNGAR

9

What we understand about Drew Brees' leadership is not that he is perfect, but rather that he is consistent in his character. Through wins and losses and through big errors in judgment, Brees remains true to his values of elevating others and showing compassion in all cir-cumstances and with all people. Even when he is in a negative spotlight. We see him consistently dedicated to learning from mistakes and using those moments as fuel for growth and unity among teams and communities. It's because of this consistency that teammates feel able to work through challenges with him, rally around him when he has misstepped, and trust his vision for their success. We saw this ring true in the aftermath of his statement when fellow athletes acknowledged his poor judgment and offered to help educate him.

Bonus Characteristic: Credibility

What I love about Lauer and Blue's article on The Three C's is that there is a plot twist and they don't stop with just three C's. An effective team captain that exhibits all of these characteristics, they conclude, establishes credibility, which ultimately translates into authenticity alongside consistency. Credibility is arguably the most valuable quality a team leader needs to have in order to have others work alongside them or follow their lead. Without it, a team leader won't have the support and sustainability needed to grow. We should be careful, too, to recognize that credibility does not necessarily mean credentials, although there is usually some overlap. You'll recall that I previously mentioned book smarts can only take you so far, but that emotional intelligence takes you across the finish line. For us, credibility teeters both of those.

This seems like a given when it comes to leadership (subject matter experts rise to the top in their fields for a reason), but the reality of this looks a bit different in practice, doesn't it? Have you worked for a manager in your career who you believed didn't know what they were doing and who you were more qualified than for the task at hand? Have you ever found yourself not wanting to collaborate with another team member or team leader because you didn't trust their judgment would provide effective value for the task at hand? It's likely you've felt this way because at some point, they demonstrated a lack of expertise or credibility to you in one form or another, which has caused you to become apathetic toward the project and/or apprehensive toward working with them. If this is something you relate to, I encourage you to challenge your definition of credibility and consider that credibility is more about trust than subject matter expertise.

*****

There is a common understanding of the types of (what I will call) skills a leader should have: communication, organization, presentation skills, etc. Many books and resources aim to outline these and provide tools to induce and strengthen these required skills, but what I aim to achieve in this book is to look more fundamentally at what makes those skills possible. Before we get to skill-building in our career (like organization and communication), which are more operational, we have to step back and address the behaviors and mindset that make skillsets work together effectively. I liken this concept to that of the human brain and white matter. White matter is the glue that holds the various functions together (gray matter), allowing them to properly interact with and react to one another. White matter is the transmitter, so to speak. If we take this example and apply it to how we think about skill-building and character attributes, skills like communication (gray matter areas) are held together by white matter characteristics and attributes, which produce the output of activities, mindset and behaviors. This book aims to address the white matter attributes and characteristics that create a more solidified and functional leader through behaviors and mindsets, which skills like communication and organizational complement and manifest.

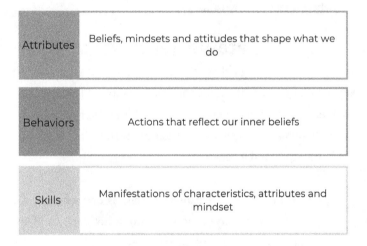

Attributes	Beliefs, mindsets and attitudes that shape what we do
Behaviors	Actions that reflect our inner beliefs
Skills	Manifestations of characteristics, attributes and mindset

The Three C's (and bonus characteristic) is just one lens to look through when identifying the glue or white matter that holds attributes together, but it's one of my favorites because it forces us to look at what seems so obvious and simple, but often can get lost in translation when applied to the business world. As we continue in this book, keeping these four characteristics top of mind will enable us to see how these three foundational characteristics and attributes translate into daily behaviors and activities, which then translates into skills, that foster true "team" environments and effective leaders. The Three C's here are a practical way of looking through the moral intelligence lens. Most know, or at least have heard of "emotional intelligence", but here we go beyond this and consider integrity, responsibility, sympathy and more. Keeping commitments, maintaining our integrity and being authentic are outputs of moral intelligence and they directly reflect how we most inwardly behave and feel—and *that* is how we teach those around us to behave and feel when interacting with us.

Tweetable Takeaways

Let's get social! Being able to share your growth along the way is key to transparency as a leader and building other leaders as you go. Here are important takeaways from this chapter that you can easily share on social using #LeadershipFromATeamCaptain and my handle @CiaraUngar.

- A team leader above anything else is one who sets the tone and (ideally) a good example for the rest of the team to show up and do their best.
- Caring is first and foremost the number one characteristic of a team captain, and it goes beyond just caring for the members of the team themselves and extends to their care and passion for the work they do.
- Being a courageous team captain means having the integrity to walk the talk and willingness to step up to the task at hand.

- It takes less courage to redirect blame onto others for failure, than it does to put ourselves on equal footing at the risk of losing our merit.
- A consistent team captain is not only consistent with their character from person to person, but is consistent through all circumstances, even when others are not knowingly watching.
- Captains are a model of consistency, or more simply put, authenticity.
- Consistency as a leader must be about who you are everyday during trials and wins, on and off the field.

3

UNLEARNING PERFECTION

unlearning an invisible ideal

erfection is hands down one of the most difficult topics to tackle when it comes to leadership and professional development because it's so engrained in who we are as a society and how we define success. This notion of perfection is at the root of a lot of conflict in the workplace due to the varying degrees of weight placed on and definitions given to *perfection*, so starting here will uncover several misconceptions and align us as we head into other discussions throughout this book.

What comes to mind when you think of perfection?

For most, perfection means an error-free output. Is that what came to mind for you? If it did, you're in good company and probably have also struggled with feeling inadequate or

31

imperfect to a degree in nearly every role or personal relationship you've had when you've been unable to achieve this. (My inner-psychologist says: let's stop here and explore that. But, we'll move on.) Conversely, some who believe in perfection put up a façade that they are error free and hold the same standard of others, often feeling disappointed in or frustrated by others when that standard is not met. I would venture to say neither of those mentalities are healthy for us to live in and can not only impact us but also those around us.

For me, the need for perfection started when I was young. Childhood chores weren't necessarily in place to create teamwork and common ownership but rather were to teach work ethic and, frankly, to help me pull weight in a strained household. For my mother, completion usually only meant perfection. An example of this was weekend cleaning chores. Even in our single-story home, this wasn't a menial task because, as chance would have it, we had a lot of wood in our house and dusting was top of the list for my chores. When I think back on this, I can't help but chuckle because the entire kitchen floor to bottom and wood paneling throughout the house was a lot of wood to dust: wood cabinets floor to ceiling, wood floors, wooden baseboards, wooden baskets on the countertops, wooden paneling on the walls through the common areas, wooden table, wooden railing, wooden furniture… and the list goes on. Needless to say, "dusting" was the worst chore you could have been assigned.

I've never really talked about this as an adult (mostly because I think I've forgotten it until it has a reason to come up), but to think back on having to do this as an adolescent has revealed a number of implications it has had on who I became as an athlete, adult, and professional. In a way, chores are meant to teach kids responsibility and management of their lives—to take care of your things and stay disciplined. As a kid, I did my own laundry often, managed my homework, usually had a decently cleaned room with bed made (not *always* by any means), had perfect attendance by the time I graduated high school, worked two jobs during high school, never missed a soccer, cheerleading or softball practice or game, was class president, team captain and I maintained good grades. I worked hard and aimed for perfection often. The chores given achieved their purpose in teaching me self-responsibility and dedication—invaluable lessons I wouldn't change for the world because it paved the way for professional growth and success I wouldn't otherwise have been prepared for. As much as it paved a way of dedication, however, I can see that it also subconsciously engrained an expectation that was a mirage that has been the source of a lot of professional tension. My work ethic is one of my strongest attributes as a professional and I acknowledge the foundation childhood chores and perfection created for success. But, there's another element to this self-discipline that I've spent many years dissecting and unlearning, which can be a controversial topic.

For many, we look at successful leaders like Steve Jobs, who only believed in perfection, and it paid off quite well for both him and the ecosystem he built that is now embedded into the majority of people's lives. In many ways, I understand what Jobs was looking to achieve because I've struggled for much of my career in the same way, holding myself and others to a standard of "perfect." To this day, I often feel haunted when I think back to some of the horrendous ways I have interacted with those I've managed in holding them to a false standard that isn't possible. If you interviewed some of these colleagues from my past, many would say without hesitation that I'm a perfectionist, which I've seen take a toll on work environments and team dynamics. Not only would tension arise, but the quality of work became affected because of demotivation and a broken process that didn't consider each person's unique talents and ways of working. I've taken great care to since reflect on this as a leader and take steps to mend those relationships and dynamics, actively unlearn this mindset and replace it with positive mentality and behavior not grounded in achieving perfection—because it simply doesn't exist. Before you judge, I know I'm not alone in falling into the trap that "perfect" is what we must achieve and anything less isn't acceptable, and that's because it's how we have been raised as a society.

Going back to the one-story home I grew up in that had (what felt like) an excess amount of wood in it... More often than not, I would have to dust this wood more than once before it was considered good enough to be complete. Rarely did I put in less than 100% effort (affectionately referred to in my family now as the "half asked" effort) because I knew I would have to redo the work repeatedly if it wasn't *perfect*. Even so, I would have to redo the work if it didn't meet standard—two times, three times, maybe even four times. Without a doubt, it was activities like this as a kid that led me to internalize the requirement for perfection, regardless of effort or intention, and I carried this standard into adulthood and into my professional career to a fault.

Historically, I held team members to the same standard I held myself to—that of perfection. My style was usually that of pushing individuals to do their best, and some colleagues really embraced this while others grew only to despise me for it. I've come to realize as I've worked through collaborative environments, matured as a leader and led many teams since that a standard of perfection can also tear teams apart and is rooted in something that doesn't exist. I've seen that it not only reduces morale and demotivates, the unachievable standard of perfection also damages a leader's relationship with his or her team, tarnishes trust and creates an obstacle to harmony. Unfortunately, it took a life-altering circumstance for me to see that pushing others to do their best doesn't always have to mean perfection, nor does perfection always equate to error-free, and that above all, showing empathy and collaboration gets you closer to perfection than any other behavior could:

In late Fall 2017, I was diagnosed with late-stage Neurological Lyme Disease with Carditis. The sudden deterioration of my cognitive and physical abilities at the time was difficult to work through and taught me many important lessons. One of which was the importance of teamwork and definition of perfection. The team I was working with at the time had no reason to rally behind me the way they did, and I'm quite certain they'll never know how appreciative I am of their support during that experience. Before getting sick, I was known for being difficult to work with because of my standard of perfection and the strain it placed on collaborative tasks. When my ability to function was stripped from me (what seemed like) overnight, I had no choice but to change my definition of perfection and rely on my teammates to show grace where I failed to show grace to myself.

Without this grace, I experienced what I'm sure many have experienced a time or two:

- Feeling morally obligated to over-deliver and failing to meet this meant I was morally failing.
- Designating everything as worthy of full effort when I physically couldn't give that left me feeling inadequate.
- Feeling annoyed if I couldn't give 100% to a habit created a lack of flexibility and prevented new projects from starting.
- The list goes on...

I share this story because learning to show myself (and others) grace has been part of my professional development journey, particularly my relationship to perfection and how I define leadership. Until I didn't have a choice, I thought perfection was a choice for all and a reflection of effort and skill. One of the most important lessons I have since learned is that there is a distinction to be made between excellence and perfection. Excellence creates the opportunity for growth and improvement, wherein one is always striving to do their best work. It is excellence that has a positive drive and allows us to work toward an end goal without the fear of failure. Perfection sets us up for failure and arguably can stunt growth and productivity. The driver for perfectionism is negative as it aims to avoid failure rather than aims to achieve growth. (A notion of "moving toward" vs "moving away" as part of our subconscious programming that I speak on in other publications.)

Many companies have embraced failure in the new-age workplace as a critical step in growth and innovation—the concept of 'failing fast' might sound familiar to you if you're in knowledge work. Why? Because when we fail, our perspective changes. Failure allows us to look beyond the end result and focus on what we can learn in the journey and process of getting there (something we saw from Drew Brees). Commitment to excellence rather than perfection opens the door for failure and flexibility, which allows us to produce greater long-term results.

With this in mind, I've often thought back to when I was on teams in the past and how these dynamics illustrated the distinction between perfection and excellence. I was fortunate enough to be part of amazing sports teams with athletes who excelled in their field. I had amazing coaches that trained us how to handle pivots and overcome defeat. When we won, we would debrief on what we did well and what we could have done better. When we lost, we did the same thing. We were never penalized for losing a game per se (as long as you don't count a few extra suicide drills at practice the next day), but rather were pushed to build on the individual strengths and weaknesses that led to those wins and losses. We were trained how to pivot our plays and moves under various scenarios, which only could have been exposed through losses and unplanned events. No single player was perfect. But, we were prepared to supplement one another's strengths and weaknesses and together worked toward excellence, not perfection. When we lost, we still won because we identified the growth opportunities that came from those losses and only paved the way for greater success.

Tweetable Takeaways

Let's get social! Being able to share your growth along the way is key to transparency as a leader and building other leaders as you go. Here are important takeaways from this chapter that you can easily share on social using #LeadershipFromATeamCaptain and my handle @CiaraUngar.

- The unachievable standard of perfection can reduce morale and motivation and damage a leader's relationship with his or her team.
- "Failure" allows us to look beyond the end result and focus on what we can learn in the journey and process of getting there.
- Commitment to excellence rather than perfection opens the door for failure and flexibility, which in turn allows us to produce greater long-term results.

Part 2

Elements of Team Leadership

4

BUILDING MOTIVATION

building intrinsic next level grit
and perseverance, not just for
your teams, but within yourself

I t's hard to define motivation without requiring intrinsic characteristics and attributes to first be present, so I feel now is a good time to introduce it in this book. How *can* you define motivation? Better yet, how would you define someone who motivates others? Is it the person on stage giving an inspirational speech receiving applause? Is it the person leading the calls or meetings at work every day? Before you answer this, I want to step back and reflect on what comes to my mind when I think of motivation and leadership. As a team captain, *motivation* has a lot of meaning and weight that is rooted deep in the person themselves. It's the part of the human that drives when external challenges arise. Let's take my experience in soccer as an example:

It's the middle of summer in Indiana where the July humidity can be taxing on your body, making it challenging to do simple tasks…like breathing (insert the dramatics). While many were enjoying their summer breaks, going on vacations or doing summer work, others were preparing for the upcoming sports season. For soccer, this meant attending "two-a-days", where there were two practices held each day (morning and evening) for the weeks prior to the start of regular practices for the season. Each practice in the day had its own focus—endurance, skill-building, teamwork, and so forth. Even for the most chiseled athlete, the difficulty during two-a-days was that their body was so exhausted from the rigor of the practices themselves, but also from the humidity they're fighting to breathe and stay hydrated through. Our morning practices were focused on building strength and endurance, usually in a humid 100+ degrees at 7:30 in the morning. Rain or shine, we would show up with our bodies dragging and in pain from the day (and weeks) before, ready to push our bodies through the weight of the heat.

During these practices, I learned what being a team captain meant and the impact of that leadership for the rest of the season. During the season, it was about keeping the team focused and harmonious during games, avoiding discouragement and making the right calls. (Picture Megan Rapinoe, Women's Soccer World Cup Champion, clapping at her teammates as she's sprinting down the field, motivating them to keep going.) During two-a-days, however, a team captain had to step into bigger shoes to go above and beyond their perceived limits. They were expected to rise above and keep the team motivated throughout practice when they themselves felt like giving up. At 7:30 am, after weeks of pushing your body in extreme heat when your body wants to give in during what feels like an outer body experience, the team captain had to rise above that pain, clap their hands and say, "keep it up, team, we're almost there" as if they felt no pain themselves. I remember those moments so vividly even today, seeing my teammates to the left and right of me as we sprinted from line-to-line on the soccer field worn physically and mentally, knowing as the captain I had to keep them motivated and couldn't show signs of defeat within myself.

This level of motivation is something I realized exists deep within who we are as people, and was engrained as a foundation in who I am from my days as an athlete. We've all heard of grit, endurance and strength, and that's what occurs when the going gets tough. But what about when the going gets even tougher? After we've pushed ourselves to our max and endured hurdle after hurdle, and then suddenly it gets even harder... what do we call *that*?

Actually, there *is* a word for it coined by the Fins and it's *Sisu*, described as determination, purpose, grit, bravery, resilience and hardness. It's a special strength and persistent determination and resolve to continue and overcome in the moment of adversity. I've seen it described as an almost magical quality: a combination of stamina, perseverance, courage and determination held in reserve for difficult times.[10] I find this definition of resilience and motivation to be fascinating, but also one that is required of leaders because of its deep roots in who we *are*, not what we can achieve, our title, or how we show up.

This scenario isn't just relatable to the athletes of the world. The workplace environment can be just as rigorous and often is. You may not be lacing up your cleats and sprinting from one painted line to another, but you are going non-stop, working through sprints, chasing goals, facing discouraging conversations, overcoming hurdles and having to work as a team to keep one another moving. I am not suggesting that running your body into overdrive like many do is healthy by any means, and in fact I believe part of leadership is helping to manage that type of environmental strain. Nonetheless, over time these rigorous days can take a toll on your body and your mind and this is where the team captains of the world, the leaders, come into play.

Good leaders lead by example in challenging environments and, in doing so, also inspire others around them to do the same. Exhibiting unwavering passion and enthusiasm for working toward the goal and what you are doing (even when it's taken everything out of you) will make others much more likely to follow your lead and also feel enthusiastic and passionate. This is where the infamous "rally cry" comes into action. Whether the team is winning or losing in its own sense, a good team captain, a good leader, must demonstrate optimism and inspire hope. Further, they should be doing so not as a façade they're putting up, but because of real motivation hosted within themselves (more on this later).

"Rallying" can look different for different teams and as a leader, it's up to you to identify what those rallying moments look like for your teams. I've practiced this in different ways over the years, depending on the environment and the team's purpose. The first team I ever managed was a team who, for one month out of every year, had to undergo turnover of apartments working a grueling 12+ hours under high physical (and emotional) demand. Until you've lived through this, it is hard to understand how demanding this month can be on the physical and mental body and the staff living through it. As a leader, it was my job during these times to not only keep myself in check while managing operations, but also to keep the rest of the team motivated and positive (something I was still learning how to do as a young leader). One way I went about this was starting each morning off with an inspirational quote—sometimes serious, sometimes funny, which I asked one person to volunteer to read each morning before we started our days. I know for most this was an annoying task they didn't want to do at 6:30 in the morning, but great benefits came from this morning routine. Inspirational quote takeaway aside, it invited team members to come together and participate in motivating others around them. The simple act of breaking up the monotony of coming into the office and starting the work allowed the team to laugh together in the morning, bond over a mantra, and rally one another and it had lasting benefits throughout the day they likely didn't realize. I've carried this tactic throughout my career, often establishing routine meetings or habits of celebrating successes and offering team members a piece of the rallying cry pie.

But… and this is a big *but*… these rallying moments only work when you've dedicated time throughout the year in those other more mundane moments building a solid foundation of motivation—not just with those around you, but for yourself. An athlete doesn't step onto the court for their first game when the season starts. They train months in advance and build muscle, technique and stamina. Leadership motivation should be considered no different. It's a muscle that we must build off the court so that when game time arrives, we've created the stamina and strength within us to show up the way we need to. Although tactics will vary, there are general approaches to building a foundation of motivation that tap into the subconscious and conscious portions of our minds.

Remove Demotivating Factors

First, extract the weeds that prevent healthy growth within your team. "Weeds" does not necessarily mean people, but rather the activities and habits we allow to enter the physical and mental space. It's the role of the team leader to ensure a harmonious working relationship within and across the entire team, helping to resolve issues and tensions. This is a critical first step to creating a foundation for motivation because a team can only work effectively if it maintains an environment free from tension and strain. Now, this can get tricky and, in many cases, Human Resources should be brought into the mix to help appropriately address elevated strains and tensions. I would pose, though, that strains and tensions usually only become elevated when they've had room to grow. This is where I believe a leader comes in observing, listening and eliminating. They should act as a team sounding board, listen and help redirect negative thinking of teammates toward positive outcomes. (Emotional intelligence plays a key role here.) Rumors or negative narratives of others on the team can spread, and the focus on positive goals can become derailed. It's important for team leaders to avoid fostering an environment where negative sentiments (weeds) are allowed to spread.

Negative relationships and tensions among the team are just one area of demotivation. Micromanagement is another common factor in demotivation among teams. Although many who micromanage may have good intentions, micromanagement can cause apathy of team members, creating a sense of insufficiency and insecurity. It demonstrates distrust in decision-making and capabilities, which often leaves the team member feeling inadequate for the position, often causing turnover. I'm guilty of micromanaging in my career, and there is certainly a time and place when it can be appropriate. More often than not, micromanaging has more negative consequences than positive effects. Generally, micromanagers have more strained relationships with their teams which can often be debilitating.

Another demotivating factor on teams can be their faith in senior leadership and where their company at large may be headed. Earlier in this book, we talked about the psychology of leadership and differences in generations, which glossed over the importance of today's workforce needing to align with the leadership they work for and the company's ethics and values. A major demotivating factor for today's teams concerns whether people see themselves aligning with the company, which can change over time. Think about how often we see colleagues (and ourselves) starting a role with great enthusiasm that then dwindles as the days go on. Often, losing enthusiasm is not just due to burnout, but also a realization that the decisions you see your leadership making may not align with your values. Over time, credibility and trust become lost, and once this faith in leadership is tarnished, loyalty withers and motivation dwindles. As a leader, removing doubt and misalignment by keeping teams aligned with the greater vision (and being a conduit to leadership of team values) is critical to fostering an environment that keeps teams motivated.

Give Recognition

Recognition is one key area that goes wildly undervalued in the workplace and can be a game-changer for employee performance. We all say "great job" and "thank you" to the group in a meeting occasionally and many companies give out bonuses in effort to show appreciation, but how often do you have a manager who goes out of their way to say thank you and acknowledge what you've done directly without prompt? There is merit to pushing your teams to strive for excellence consistently, but failing to acknowledge progress of a team as well as individual contributions can demotivate staff, cause high turnover and ultimately slow your growth as a company. What I'm *not* talking about here is giving out an award for every person and devaluing the sentiment. (Think of the 'every kid gets a trophy' argument, which has its function in childhood development and can serve a positive purpose.) What I *am* talking about is setting your own desire for recognition aside and lifting up your team. (Ultimately, their success is your success, right?) Great team leaders are not interested in personal glory and instead look for ways to serve their teams and help them accomplish their goals. Rather than focusing on what can give you credit and recognition, focus on building your team up and the rest will follow.

I recognize we are human. Everyone likes to be recognized when they put forth an effort, whether it's expected effort or not. At the beginning of this book, I talked about the psychological phenomenon of subconsciously seeking approval from our managers as parental figures. The need for recognition falls in that same vein. The words "Thank You" at the end of a busy day or hectic week can go a long way with staff and encourage them to continue in that effort. Further, sending a group email or Slack message saying "thanks everyone" or giving your staff an extra day off is a good start, but is only a small piece of showing appreciation and giving recognition. Those habits are nice and should remain part of the gratitude mix, but a concerted effort to show the *individual* you are noticing their specific contributions and are thankful for them will take you even further. Example: *"Alice, I see how you've been proactively organizing our files, and this has been very beneficial to our efficiency as a team. Thank you for being proactive, it's appreciated."* Notice how this is intentional, direct and aware? The best way to illustrate the impact of this simple act is by adapting what psychologists for ages have been encouraging troubled couples to do. When couples have entered a lull in their relationship and feel unappreciated (a common hurdle in many long-term relationships), therapists will often have couples go through an exercise of stating specifically what the spouse or partner does that the other is grateful for. This is because spoken words have a lot of power when creating positive behavior and mindsets. As humans, even the most independent individuals crave acknowledgment, and the more specific recognition is, the more we reprogram our mind and feel appreciated.

To expand on this concept a bit, I want to offer a humorous, yet real, anecdote of how I see this manifest in real scenarios. Showing appreciation seems to be an unspoken expectation, but it's often not practiced effectively. I have to look no further than my own experience to demonstrate this. A former company of mine did not value employee recognition—not in the way I'm describing it here, at least. Showing individual recognition to my colleagues was something I had adopted as a practice well before starting with this company and had intended to carry it over in the new role and team. Besides showing gratitude in most emails when work was being passed through for review, I would make a concerted effort on a bi-weekly basis (or more) to send a Slack message, text, or email expressing my gratitude for the extra hours put in that I had noticed, the attention to detail that had been evident, or other similar qualities that make a valuable teammate. I set out to proactively acknowledge and reward these behaviors and strengths when I saw them present and show my appreciation for the members of my team, illuminating what I had noticed specific to their behavior. In an environment where gratitude was never expressed, these messages were often met with awkward confusion on how to respond. After I had parted ways with the company, I had team members express how much those moments of gratitude meant to them when it was the only "thank you" they had received in the day ... or week ... or even the duration of their employment with the company. I see gratitude as a particularly critical component of being in a larger organization where you can often feel invisible and disposable.

The takeaway here is that gratitude goes a long way, but it's not always comfortable. Sometimes, the recipient of gratitude will be conditioned to negative leadership and they may not know how to respond, reciprocate or internalize. Equally, until you've mastered the practice and made it a second-nature habit, it can feel uncomfortable to extend gratitude, especially in an era with a lot of boundaries around what is appropriate. Whether you're giving recognition or receiving recognition, it takes practice to build this muscle and approach, just like any other skill you want to build.

Showing recognition is low cost with high impact. In doing so, you will produce more top performers with simple recognition than skill-building workshops ever could simply because of the motivation produced. In the words of Dvorak and Mann: "Workplace recognition motivates, provides a sense of accomplishment and makes employees feel valued for work."[11] A leader can, and should, give as much recognition as is deserved. There is no such thing as too much recognition if it's valid and honest.

Create Trust & Growth through Empowerment

Empowerment is an important factor in motivating teams. When we look at habits like micromanaging, we can see how important empowerment really is to an individual's motivation. A leader, more often than not, comes into their role because of their subject matter expertise (or at least let's hope that's the case). Although sometimes this isn't the case, they usually earn their role because they've spent years perfecting their craft and can impart that wisdom in the function of overseeing others. This natural progression of career growth often produces ego attached with the need to control. Enter micromanagement.

I mentioned earlier in this book that micromanagement does have benefits, such as ensuring quality and consistency; but there are more dangers to micromanagement than benefits, one of which is the loss of trust—some forget this is a two-way street. I recall my own experience with micromanagers I have had in my career and how deeply inadequate I felt when that behavior occurred. With one manager in particular (notice I say manager here), it had become clear quite quickly that they did not trust me to complete the work (at least the way they wanted me to) and rather than motivating me, the micromanaging behavior created apathy for the role and company. I also felt a broken trust between my manager, which created tension that only fermented over time. Unfortunately, this experience is all too common, yet completely avoidable with communication and trust that empowers. When a team lead micromanages, they risk burning themselves out, losing team innovation and creating tension; but, more importantly, there will also eventually be the breakdown of trust, which leads to a decline in productivity and employee loyalty. Perhaps even more relative to our discussion in this chapter is that micromanagement creates dependence rather than enabling team members to learn and grow.

> *Because we are each unique, we think differently. We talk differently. We react differently. We are different.[12] So, before you micromanage, stop and ask yourself: is it wrong, or is it different?*

Assuming the best of your employees and trusting them as mature, responsible contributors to the overall goal and team progress will set a foundation for motivation and trust. Stepping back and allowing team members to make their own decisions (and mistakes) will communicate that you do trust them and believe in their capabilities, even if it results in a failed attempt the first try or a different result than what you expected. Showing this trust and respect for their ability to navigate makes your job easier, but also empowers them to think on their own and learn from their own mistakes which only strengthens their ability as a teammate. You may ask: What happens if they hit a roadblock? What if it doesn't get done the way I want it to? First, be coaching your teams throughout the year on how to work through challenges and decisions, including making yourself accessible and available for help when needed. Second, give them the autonomy to achieve results in their own way to foster innovation. Before you micromanage, ask yourself this: *is it wrong, or is it different?*

Tweetable Takeaways

Let's get social! Being able to share your growth along the way is key to transparency as a leader and building other leaders as you go. Here are important takeaways from this chapter that you can easily share on social using #LeadershipFromATeamCaptain and my handle @CiaraUngar.

- *Sisu* is a special strength and persistent determination and resolve to continue and overcome in the moment of adversity.
- Good leaders lead by example in these environments and moments and, in doing so, also inspire others around them to do the same.
- Rally cry moments only work when you've dedicated time throughout the year to building a solid foundation of motivation.
- A critical first step is to extract the weeds that prevent healthy growth in your team - the activities and habits that we allow to enter the space.
- A team can only work effectively if it maintains an environment free from individual tensions.
- A good captain acts as a team sounding board, listens and helps direct negative thinking of teammates toward positive goals.
- Micromanagers tend to have more strained relationships with their teams which can often be debilitating.
- Recognition is one key area that goes wildly undervalued in the workplace and can be a game changer for employee performance.

- Showing recognition is low cost with high impact.
- Stepping back and allowing team members to make their own decisions will communicate that you do trust them and believe in their capabilities, even if it results in a failed attempt the first try.

5

BUILDING HARMONY

the relationship between
individual parts of a whole
that creates balance

This chapter was possibly my favorite to write in this book, not because it has more or less value than any other, but because I love thinking about the concept of teamwork and how great leaders foster it. For much of my younger career, the concept of teamwork was difficult for me to grasp, even with my background in sports. Teamwork in sports made sense but only mid-career did I begin to see the parallel of it in the workplace. As obvious as it sounds, the reality is we are programmed as adults to begin thinking of our own self-interest and the notion of teamwork becomes a distant thought. Consequently, it's an area of leadership that is easy to overlook and misinterpret the meaning of when we get too ahead of ourselves and our growth. For years, I was guilty of wanting to own all aspects of a project – to control the outcome, earn recognition, and I'm sure for several other reasons - and struggled to "relinquish *control*," especially in areas where I knew I could perform. As a marketing professional, I am dynamic because of my diverse background and typically can jump into each function within the marketing umbrella as needed, which has made it difficult for me to know when to handover work and step away. As I've matured, however, the concept of "we" evolved in its meaning and I came to understand the value of leading teams whose unique strengths and weaknesses—when integrated—worked well together. The greatest illustration for integrated teamwork I have come across has been that of a soccer team.

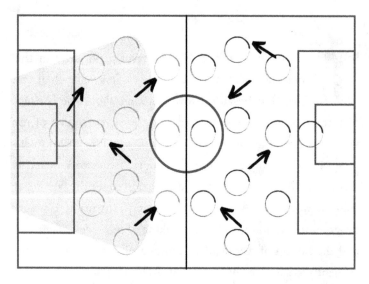

In this illustration, we can see how each team member, although functioning in their own post, is just one piece of a fully integrated team working toward a goal. Each player's skill-set balances one another as they cross-communicate, share vantage points, hand over control at the certain points where others are better positioned, and strategically think about how they compose and deliver.

I was a Right Defender in soccer, trained to anticipate movement of the opposing team from a full-field line of view. For those who know the game, the unique benefit of the goalie and defenders is that they have the unique vantage point of seeing everyone else on the field most of the time and can strategize their movements and communicate to teammates where to move the ball. If you've ever watched professional soccer on television or even played the sport, cross-functional teamwork is the centerpiece of a winning team. It seems like a given in any sport and many profess to believe in teamwork without understanding it—it has more depth to it than 'everyone gets the ball.' If you have the time, take a few hours to watch the most recent World Cup and note how little time each player actually spends with the ball when they are passing it. You'll find that each player handles the ball for just seconds (or less), usually often just touching the ball once as a pass to someone else. This synchronized and strategic movement is possible because these teams have spent hours practicing together, running plays, strategizing moves and can seamlessly move the ball down the field well. It's inspirational to watch and as leaders, we should strive to create that same harmony among our teams at work. But, it takes a little bit of homework and a lot of practice.

A team captain should know each one of their teammates and their strengths and weaknesses within the larger picture—knowledge that comes from studying playback video, observing, having one-on-one discussions (which I'll talk more on a little later), and taking the time to understand each player. They know how each individual reacts to high-pressure situations and who can be leveraged in complicated plays vs. who can be counted on for more steady-paced relays. It is the job of the team captain to pull his or her team together based on those skills (not fit them into a box of sameness), knowing where one player will burn out and where another will best supplement. This approach to leadership creates a function for each team member that allows for spontaneous and harmonious movements that will position the team to produce the greatest opportunity to score.

This same principle can be applied to leading a team with diverse skills sets in the workplace. Much like a team captain, the leader should study the skills of his or her team members, recognize who is capable of what, get familiar with their movements, and try to adjust their "gameplay" accordingly. For winning soccer teams, the strategy is never about giving the most skilled player the most ball time, but rather building a team that can—with a single touch—make an appropriate move that sets another team member up for success (or move the ball into scoring position so to speak). The winning component of this approach is not that each player has the same qualities (something I believe the notion of "company culture" often promotes), but rather each player's unique qualities are appropriately applied.

But creating team harmony goes beyond simply knowing what skills to leverage and when. As a leader, creating a harmonious team that maintains its focus (and motivation) is done by rallying behind each member both in good times and in bad. A leader has the unique responsibilities of living by example (mentioned throughout the last few chapters), especially for creating harmony. If you want your team to maintain focus and stay calm under pressure, this is how you must also carry yourself. This includes rallying behind your team members when they've made a mistake or fallen short of the ideal result. I have observed with many teams how easy it can be to get caught up in ostracizing others because of a personality trait or perceived skill shortcoming and sometimes there is merit to why people feel the way they do. As a team leader, however, it's our job to take the first step in rallying around the team member who didn't meet the expectations of others to hold the team together, keeping everyone focused on the goal at hand and not a single individual. A good team leader doesn't show favoritism or promote cliques but looks for ways to create a positive attitude, which goes a long way to fostering an environment that breeds success.

In a later chapter, I discuss conflict resolution, which—when done well—can build team harmony. Creating a team with a good ebb and flow isn't as black and white, however. There's not a right way to structure your team to ensure all areas are covered. Sure, you can hire for each skill you think you may need to fulfill, but having all skills represented is not harmony. After all, we are more than just skills... we are humans with emotions, perceptions, habits and ways of life. All of these factors make us who we are in the workplace and shape how we function on any given team. There are, however, ways you can strengthen your team to create the agility and harmony to best position your team for success. Harmony is about how a team moves together despite any particular set of skills at play. It's about the personality and character fostered as a unit. Harmony in music, as Master Class puts it, is the element that can "elevate a piece from common and predictable to challenging and sophisticated."[13] It's the *relationship* between individual parts that balance one another. Harmony among teams is no different and it's something that takes time (and practice) to develop. I firmly believe you cannot simply hire new talent to fill a skill gap and achieve harmony. I do believe, though, that you can practice and build harmony over time with habit-forming activities and accountability. Really, much of what we discuss in this entire book—building trust, communication, consistency, motivation and so on—all work toward creating harmony among a team. As a leader, though, it's important to make a conscious effort to create harmony just as you would aim to achieve other growth and skills goals.

- Define Collaboration. Believe it or not, not everyone views collaboration the same. For some, collaboration can mean not disagreeing on the same direction. For others, collaboration can mean disagreeing but conceding to one side. I reject both of those ideals of collaboration even though collaboration can lead to both of those outcomes. I believe it's about listening to varying perspectives and translating the most impactful elements of those insights into one integrated solution. It's not about each side arguing their side until one is picked, but a true combination of the best elements. I love the analogy Liefeld offers: One person can believe the Chicago Cubs (Go Cubs Go!) are the best team, and another can believe the White Sox are the best team. Both can be right and, again, just because someone's opinion is different doesn't mean it's wrong. Whether or not this is your definition of collaboration, I've found it's important to define collaboration on your teams so there is a baseline if you wish everyone to practice it. If we are to say that collaboration creates harmony, we can't assume everyone aligns on what that looks like. So, to pursue harmony on your teams, an exercise that aligns with a co-created definition of what it means and looks like for your team will create a consistent expectation they feel empowered to uphold. Teach your teams how to discuss and debate outside of reaching easy consensus. Discussing and deciding on alternative ideas and approaches in pursuit of the best outcome is how you'll effectively create collaboration.

- Create Balance. Harmony is really about the balance of movement, and for teams to have balance interdependently, they must feel supported in having balance individually. In Maura Nevel Thomas's book, *Work Without Walls*, she talks about knowledge work and various ways we easily create burnout. For many of us, we're in the heart of knowledge work and our mind is our tool. Ensuring we reboot, rest and reset that tool is one of the greatest factors of success, including working well with others. I encourage you to read this book and assess how you, as the leader, can create balance for your team members so they can balance one another.

- Define Team Conduct. Harmony is also about how teams carry themselves and respect one another. In sports, we have flags, penalties, and fouls with clearly defined rules around what those look like. I'm not suggesting that you immediately penalize your teams when they violate codes of conduct (although certain circumstances warrant it), but I *am* suggesting you work through a team exercise that allows the team to define their expectations for how they should be treated by their colleagues and vice versa. When teams can define for themselves what they expect from their teammates, they're more likely to hold themselves accountable to the same standard. Ask them questions, such as: *how do they define what respect looks and sounds like*; *what do they value out of colleagues and a workplace,* and *what does positive communication look like?*

- Identify Personalities. One of the most collaborative and effective agencies I have been a part of started each new hire with a few books to read, which included communication styles and personality trait assessments. The goal of this was to get to know how each employee preferred to communicate and where they fit in the team's output. It also reinforced that people have different ways of working through projects and information, which can impact how projects and timelines are structured and what expectations there are. I have found this to be very critical to removing "weeds" and toxic rumors. In knowledge work, there can be certain personalities that do well in certain areas or phases of creation, but more important, different teams work well together because of the ebb and flow balance of their personality. Knowing where your team members fit as personalities can help to create harmony and balance.

Tweetable Takeaways

Let's get social! Being able to share your growth along the way is key to transparency as a leader and building other leaders as you go. Here are important takeaways from this chapter that you can easily share on social using #LeadershipFromATeamCaptain and my handle @CiaraUngar.

- Teamwork is the centerpiece to a winning team.
- A team captain knows each one of its teammates and their strengths and weaknesses within the larger picture.
- Harmony is about how a team moves together despite any particular set of skills at play.
- As a leader it's important to make a conscious effort to create harmony: Define collaboration, create balance, define team conduct, identify personalities.

6

YOUR ONE-ON-ONE GAME

individual relationships strengthen
the trust of the larger team
and your leadership

"I nterpersonal skills" is tough to tackle in one setting,
because great interpersonal skills don't come naturally for many and require discipline and training to
build and maintain. So much so, there are even college majors
dedicated to building interpersonal skills. So, if this is an area
you've struggled with as a leader, don't be discouraged as you're
not alone. This has been one of the more difficult areas of leadership for me to master in my own career and I know that I
have many years ahead before I can master it as second nature. It
took a life-altering event for me to recognize I needed to dedicate

more of my energy toward my interpersonal relationships on my teams, or my one-on-one game if you will, because it's those individual relationships that strengthen the trust and synergy of the larger team as a whole—and it starts with you, the team captain.

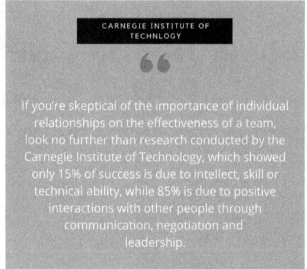

CARNEGIE INSTITUTE OF TECHNLOGY

66

If you're skeptical of the importance of individual relationships on the effectiveness of a team, look no further than research conducted by the Carnegie Institute of Technology, which showed only 15% of success is due to intellect, skill or technical ability, while 85% is due to positive interactions with other people through communication, negotiation and leadership.

14

Effective team captains take the time to get to know their teams individually on a personal level, something we can apply to the workplace. If you're not spending time with non-leadership team members, you're missing out and risk being disconnected from them. Simply taking the time to ask how they're doing every single day—face to face or on the phone—and actually listening can go a long way with your teams; but (as with everything else we've discussed so far) it goes beyond a quick drive-by as a box check. Admittedly, this is an area I have struggled with in my career because I am not much of a partier and have always upheld professional integrity at utmost importance and, for a long time, felt that hanging out outside of work was inappropriate (I'm a recovering traditionalist in that way). Growing up, I was taught there is no mixing of business and pleasure and that translated into my belief you can't have friendships with those you work with because it can blur the lines of professionalism. Although there is truth to this to a degree, it's not entirely accurate and I have experienced first-hand how detrimental it can be to have no connection with your teams outside of the office. When you take the time as a leader to get to know your team as individuals outside of the office, you can better understand their motivators, preferred communication styles and their own expectations—which begins to build rapport and trust. Trust, as we'll discuss in the next chapter, is a critical tool to establish among teams. Collaboration cannot occur without trust because a teammate has to have this trust in order to 'let go of the ball and pass.' When team members see you beyond a job title and bio, they see you outside of a closed door and feel more connected to the decisions you're making. As the team leader, it's your responsibility to ensure steps are taken to build these interpersonal relationships both between you and individual team members, and between the team members themselves.

Getting to Know Your Team
Kobe Bryant

We've talked about the importance of understanding each team member's strengths and having individual relationships to promote harmony and trust, so I want to pause here to highlight an athlete who gave us a great example of this. Kobe Bryant, a world-renown

NBA player, father, husband and a legacy in leadership, believed in the importance of understanding each of your teammates and how they contribute to the team individually. Kobe was touted by team members and coaches as—although unique and amazing in his craft—controversial at times. His leadership style varied with each team member he interacted with:

KOBE BRYANT

66

That approach never wavered..."What I did adjust, though, was how I varied my approach from player to player. I still challenged everyone and made them uncomfortable, I just did it in a way that was tailored to them."

@CIARAUNGAR

15

What Kobe understood was that being hard on everyone doesn't work. Being soft to everyone doesn't work. Instead, there is a unique combo of the two balanced in a different way for each individual because people learn differently based on their life experiences. Kobe spent significant time doing his homework on teammates, looking at how they behaved, learning their histories and trying to get to know them on a personal level. He took the extra step to hear about their goals, fears, doubts, strengths, and securities because he understood the importance of understanding them as people-first before understanding them as professionals playing ball.

We can learn a lot from Kobe and his approach. If we wish to bring out the best in our teams, we need to know what levers to pull and nerves to touch—and further, *when*. Kobe didn't mind pushing teammates to their limits because it brought out the best in them, but it started with listening and observing verbal and nonverbal behavior, not speaking *at* them and understanding an approach they'll best respond to. What we saw from Kobe was him putting personal success aside and lifting up the success of those around him, which ultimately positioned him in his own greatness. He looked at what others were feeling and doing before every game, gauging rhythm and readiness and always looking for ways he could help.

Some of the greatest examples of leadership we see across sports and business are those who know how to effectively communicate with those around them and understand their teammates outside of the game. Building trust, transparency and more all happen in our one-on-one moments and cascade out into team success—and... you guessed it... it goes beyond simply what we say to others. Getting your team pumped for the game or a new project or goal (motivation) all comes down to having good communication skills and building good rapport (trust) with them, which unfortunately can be broken in an instant (more on this later). Taking the good with the bad and doing so with balance and clarity can radiate out to your teams, fostering confidence in your decision making, reactions and ability to keep them informed. A key component of your one-on-one communication is your ability to be open to other approaches and insights, not fitting others into your ideal employee persona, and consider them as valid as your own. (It's also your ability to step away from corporate jargon and use a human voice and heart when speaking to teams.)

Resembling the Coach

An important element of building a strong rapport with your teams is to understand that a critical part of your role is to reflect the values of the company and executive teams (remember consistency and motivation?). As a team captain, your job is to resemble the "coach" (company) on a more relatable level as a conduit of their advice and instruction on how to execute plays and skills appropriately. Similarly, as a team leader, it's important to reflect the company's and/or executive team's values, processes, and vision and serve as a guide. This is, unfortunately, an area overlooked and undervalued and fails employees all too often, as people are put in leadership positions who talk poorly about the values and processes of their company or executive leadership team to their direct reports or create their own rules and processes that differ. I believe in having a discerned and innovative mind of your own as a leader, but being an effective leader also means being the conduit of information to build rapport and trust from the most senior levels to the most junior levels. If a team captain is creating a disconnect between his or her team with the rest of the company and its values, the team's motivation will deteriorate and its growth will be stunted.

I'll pause here and make a guess that some readers of this book will recall situations they've been in—whether as a leader or team member—where they've experienced this disconnect. Some may recall a boss they had who talked poorly of the executive teams or undermined the company process. Many may be reflecting on their own situations when they've taken a role with a company they didn't believe in, but the temporary discomfort propelled their career. It would be fair to ask: Are you *not* supposed to take a leadership role simply because you don't believe in the company values or align with their vision?

There isn't a straightforward answer for this, unfortunately. If we are to follow the suggestions of this book, the answer is no, don't take the role. Distrust is contagious and if you, as the team captain, don't trust *your* coach or other teammates, your team will distrust you and those around them. If you're unable to respect and trust your executive leadership or company, or if you can't authentically teach the company values, consider playing for a different team. I believe in integrity and if you don't align with the company you're working for and its values, you won't be happy there and it can and will be felt in each project and dynamic you engage in. Your alignment, or lack thereof, with a company has a rippled effect, good or bad. So, "don't work for a company you don't like" is what I would love to say in response to this question. But it may not be the most practical answer. We do have to take roles as building blocks to learn and advance in our careers (at least this will be the case with most professionals and true of at least one role in their journey).

In these circumstances, how do you go about your day resembling the company and acting as a conduit of trust and rapport, so the team you're leading isn't affected negatively? The secret: find common ground, maintain respect, and be mindful of your nonverbal communication.

Find Common Ground. You may not align with the vision of your executive leadership, but you can learn to find common ground to build from. As in other sections of this book where I recommend getting to know your team members outside of work, I'd apply the same principle here and encourage you to do the same with your executive leadership teams. As the leader, it's your role to bridge teams, and beginning by uncovering commonalities is critical. At the root of humans, we all are all mothers, fathers, sisters, brothers, neighbors, former athletes, book worms and the list goes on. Take the time to uncover those pieces of them so you can better understand their perspectives, who they are, and explore ways to build bridges. If you wish to create change, if you wish to both stand up for what you believe while also getting along with others and work toward a common goal, you must have a relationship as a foundation of trust.

Maintain Respect. It's ok to disagree with your executive teams and some decisions they make. As a leader, you're tasked with motivating your teams despite this. Let's consider an example: Your executive leadership has asked you to communicate a new policy to your teams, but you don't agree with the policy and have voiced your stance on it. Your team could easily be demotivated if they know you don't agree with the new policy and going behind the back of your upper management making your opinion known would create division and could hurt your influence in those future discussions (think back to consistency). Even if your team already knows you disagree, it's important to maintain your trust and keep them motivated. You can do this by being very conscious of how and when you're communicating the new policy: "This isn't the choice I would have made, but let's try to implement this change to the best of our abilities. We can always suggest adjustments that will make this work better than we think right now."[16] In choosing this path, you're creating the potential for growth and getting your team members on board.

Be Mindful of Nonverbals. All-too-often I have experienced leaders who will roll their eyes, sigh under their breath, and use other nonverbal cues to communicate they don't align with their executive teams. When your team members see this, they take your lead. You can use emails and speeches to convey your support, but your nonverbal communication can say much more about how you feel and it's highly contagious to those around you. In other sections of this book, I discuss the idea that if employees don't feel supported or aligned, they become unhappy at work and quit. Using nonverbal cues that encourage a disconnect and divide is dangerous territory and can hurt your team's motivation. To be a strong leader encouraging of your executive leadership, be mindful of your nonverbal cues. Be intentional about *when* and *what* you communicate to have better control over *how* you communicate—practice, create a positive environment, and use notes to keep on track.

Emotional Intelligence

Emotional Intelligence is arguably one of the most important factors to your success as a team leader and centers on the ability to know what you're feeling (as well as what others are feeling), what your emotions mean, and how these emotions can affect other people around you. Although difficult to measure, unlike one's IQ, research supports that higher EQ alongside other factors (morality, body language, etc.) is more important to a team's success than IQ alone. Emotionally intelligent teams have shown to be more productive, efficient and motivated and this is due to the trust and rapport built that sets a strong foundation for effective communication. Without EQ, environments become stressful, collaboration is hindered, and motivation dwindles.

As a leader, your level of emotional intelligence or awareness can be quite impactful to your team: your relationship with each individual, how you manage your team as a whole, and how you interact with others at large in the workplace. By maintaining a high awareness, leaders can foster safe environments that enable employees to feel comfortable enough to take calculated risks and make recommendations among their peers. Beyond direct interactions with others, emotional intelligence also means maintaining an accurate picture of his or her own strengths and weaknesses and operating from a mindset of humility regardless of a position of authority. This also means the ability to put ego aside when receiving and giving feedback to avoid creating wedges and maintain objectivity. (You can learn more about emotional intelligence for leadership at CiaraUngar.com.)

Empathy

Empathy warrants a standalone discussion because of its central role to how we interact with each other in the work place, as well as impacts perceptions, expectations and outcomes. Effective communication and team harmony cannot happen without empathy, but it can be tricky to master. So, before we talk about what it means in the workplace, I'd like to first address misconceptions of what empathy is and its importance in leadership.

> *Empathy is not Sympathy.* Empathy is often thought of as synonymous with sympathy, which is when someone feels pity or sorrow for another individual when they are polar opposites. When you feel sorrow and pity for another, it applies embarrassment to the situation, which leads to isolation. As we'll unpack in the remainder of this chapter, creating isolation is the opposite of the goal of empathy.
>
> *Empathy is not Fixing.* Contrary to what we are often taught, having empathy for someone else does not mean you are fixing their situation. Offering ways to remedy a situation can often be misconstrued and received as judgmental.

Empathy is not Liking. Have you ever found yourself in a situation where you disliked someone else, and in the midst of an unfortunate situation found it difficult to have empathy for them? A misconception of empathy is that you must like another individual to feel empathy for them; and although it's difficult to do so, liking someone is not a requisite for feeling empathy for them. Empathy is listening and hearing others out, even when you dislike them, and doing so can lead to productive and informative discussions.

Empathy is instead the ability to place yourself in someone else's shoes to understand their motivations and reasoning and consider their unique perspectives, even if you don't agree. It is a verb requiring proactive responses to create the greatest outcome in each situation and dynamic. Being an empathetic team leader takes a lot of strength and discipline; it requires you to set your emotions and opinions aside to net the best result and create fruitful dialogue without fear or judgment. It requires you to actively support the career and personal growth of your teammates.

Previously noted, sympathy and empathy often get confused for one another. More often than not, sympathy is an emotion of compassion we have for someone and their circumstance—many are born with this ability to feel pity for others. Not so innate for most is the ability to be empathetic—it usually requires practice to build this muscle. It requires research, asking questions, and trying to understand the rationale in their point of view. Empathy is going beyond sympathy and feeling and understanding the emotions and needs of those around us;

and *building* empathy among your teams is about bringing your teams together through exercises of understanding and listening.

The most successful sports teams are filled with empathy, as are the most successful companies in the world. In fact, the top ten most successful companies in the world over-index on empathy. This is because the practice of empathy creates a trusted space, which we know fosters productivity, and it's the team captain who has the unique position of ensuring it is present in every discussion both on and off the field. To aid you as a leader in building empathy across your teams, I've outlined some steps here:

- Tackle your anti-empathetic actions. This requires a level of vulnerability and honesty that isn't usually comfortable. To understand what we don't, we have to allow ourselves to truthfully identify our biases. When you look at each of your team members—what do you instantly think? Have you developed assumptions or prejudices about them? Have you concluded they have traits you perhaps don't agree with? Have you subconsciously shown favor to certain members over others? Be real with yourself in this exercise and examine why you have the biases you do. Once you've identified your biases, take the step to learn why you have them. Look at your own socializations and experiences and how they may differ from that of the other. Spend some time with your team and get to know them outside of their professional title.

- Offer constructive criticism in healthy ways. Each person has their own personality type and ways of responding to feedback. Personality types and life experiences have a major impact on how others will receive what you offer. Get to know their personality types through a variety of tools, such as Myers Briggs and DISC, and learn how to best convey feedback in a healthy way based on how they respond best to it.

- Solicit regular feedback from your teams. Checking in has a lot of advantages. We are always evolving as humans— the definition of wellness is continued evolution. Life experiences can change us in a single day and the needs of your team members can quickly change. As well-intentioned as leaders can often be, if we're not checking in to make sure we're on track with how we should be leading and with the impact we should be making, we could be heading down a path of destruction.

- Cultivate curiosity. To understand another perspective, it's important to push ourselves out of our comfort zones. Cultivating curiosity among your teams will encourage them to step out of those comfort zones and learn about, not just others on their team, but others in the world. Asking questions, visiting new places and spaces and working through improv exercises can help you and your team become comfortable with the unfamiliar.

Gendered Dynamics
Gender & Empathy

Before we move on from empathy, I feel it is important to address differences between the sexes and empathy and the unique challenges of men and women within leadership. Although I'll leave a detailed analysis for another publication, I feel it's worth discussing at the surface the topic of empathy and how this trait of a leader can (perceivably) differ between sexes. I'll caveat this aside by stating I do not support gender roles personally—men and women have equal responsibility and capability to be mindful and successful in any dynamic and applying one characteristic to an entire sex isn't a fair trial. My personal politics, however, can be separated from what decades of research and cultural institution has created a foundation of: gender roles.

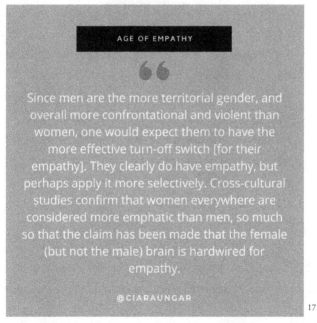

AGE OF EMPATHY

"

Since men are the more territorial gender, and overall more confrontational and violent than women, one would expect them to have the more effective turn-off switch [for their empathy]. They clearly do have empathy, but perhaps apply it more selectively. Cross-cultural studies confirm that women everywhere are considered more emphatic than men, so much so that the claim has been made that the female (but not the male) brain is hardwired for empathy.

@CIARAUNGAR

17

There is much research to support that females are more empathetic than males, but contrary to popular belief, this research rarely attributes genetics as the cause for this. Further, research shows inconclusively that there are biological traits like hormones and Oxytocin that can create greater empathy (usually found higher in females). I could go down a rabbit hole of research that supports biological differences in how each sex processes information (and how that can be impacted by gender association); however, social factors are consistently cited as one of the strongest influences that shape how empathetic a person is or how one perceives themselves to be empathetic. Females have traditionally been held at higher expectations to be understanding of others' feelings, while males have traditionally been socialized to not give in to such emotions. Regardless of your position on gender roles in the workplace, the reality and impact of this socialization over time have meant that men in leadership have a more challenging time allowing themselves to have or show empathy. Although our culture is slowly becoming more accepting and encouraging of men who openly discuss topics like mental health and empathy, we still have a long way to go before we see the disproportionate male leadership become more open to these topics without the fear of judgment or perceived weakness. Even in the case that men are naturally less empathetic, it is a trait vital to (and achievable by) both sexes regarding leadership, and it's important that men understand how to harness the portion of empathy they *are* capable of cultivating. After all, an MLB pitcher is on the team mostly to pitch while in defense, but he shouldn't neglect his hitting to support the offense. Empathy may not be a main skill of males innately (again, a generalization), but a good leader cannot afford to let it slack.

The good news is learning and embodying empathy is a challenge for both sexes alike and the tactics to developing the skill are non-binary. Although men will need to overcome deep-rooted socialized expectations, it is not impossible to learn the skill of empathy so you can become a better leader. Here are a few tactics for developing empathy as a team leader that apply to both females and males:

- ▶ Step Out of Your Comfort Zone. Developing a new skill or professional competency, undertaking a challenging experience, and experiencing different cultures and environments will not only humble you, but it will give you a greater appreciation for others.
- ▶ Ask for Feedback. Although no one will ever understand us as much as we understand ourselves, soliciting feedback from trusted colleagues, mentors, family members and friends about your relationship skills will give you an objective opinion to consider.
- ▶ Learn About Others. Cultivating a sense of curiosity means asking a lot of questions of others who are both like you and unlike you. By asking thoughtful, provocative and meaningful ques-

tions, you will develop a stronger understanding of the people around you.

▸ Walk A Mile. We've all heard the expression 'Walk a Mile in My Shoes', which is the underlying notion of empathy. To become more empathetic, we must consider what it is like in someone else's shoes and how they perceive an experience. This can often mean examining your own biases (age, race, gender, sexual preference, income level, educational background, etc.) that may interfere with your ability to listen and empathize. Every person has biases; no one is exempt. The difference in being a great leader is the ability to be aware of your own biases and not let those biases manifest or impact behavior and decision-making. A great way to overcome this is to look beyond intellectual factors and explore the hearts and mentalities of others. Conduct research and review case studies that explore personal relationships, psychology and emotions to gain a greater understanding of differing motivational factors.

Conflict Resolution

Whether you like to watch sports or not, everyone has seen their fair share of a quarrel or two on the field or court whilst watching a match on TV or in person. Often, you'll see a teammate run over to the player involved in the conflict and try to help dissolve the situation. As a team captain, this was one key responsibility and I can recall several situations when it was more difficult than others to "cool down" the team and mitigate the issues between players or players and referees. There will always be conflict in sports, just as there will always be conflict in business. We may not get as physical in the workplace as we do on the field—lest we get a visit from Human Resources—, but the nature of those situations remains quite similar and requires similar approaches to resolving conflict so we can preserve the internal and external harmony, motivation, trust and productivity of the teams. As a leader, your teams will lean on you to help resolve conflict, whether in group settings or individually and doing so effectively will improve productivity and performance.

But, as with many circumstances this is often easier said than done. Conflict can arise in many shapes and forms stemming from differences in beliefs, expectations or ideas. In an increasingly diverse workplace where professionals from all backgrounds, skill sets, attitudes, and so forth are being integrated into one team, nature tells us there will undoubtedly be conflict at some point. Constructive conflict can be healthy and, as discussed within empathy, can create fruitful outcomes of innovation and growth and bring teams closer together if navigated effectively.

Emotional intelligence plays a large role in managing conflict of your teams effectively, but it goes well beyond your own emotional intelligence in that moment. In ideal circumstance, you'll have coached your team members to talk to one another and resolve conflict on their own. This is the ideal route to conflict resolution because it removes your authority and dictation from the dynamic and enables a co-created solution that each employee can buy-into and take ownership of. When your team members own the path of the resolution, they are more likely to follow through with it. Mediation is preferred over authority, but not every conflict can be resolved this easily, and sometimes the team leader must intervene. There are courses dedicated to conflict resolution that provide a much more thorough set of tools than what can be offered in the setting of this book, but I will offer a few considerations as you consider building your conflict resolution muscle.

First, it's important to recognize that some conflicts cannot (and should not) be resolved by you, and this is ok. Sometimes, Human Resources or other authorities may have to step in, and these guidelines may differ from company to company. When elevation is unnecessary, however, conflict resolution will fall on you to effectively mediate a situation and turn it into a growth opportunity. The ultimate goal of resolving conflict is to ensure that team members can still work together effectively upon resolution, rather than creating alienation and frustration that can hinder creativity and productivity. There are many professional development books and blogs out there that outline conflict resolution steps to take, but it all points to recognizing, respecting and appreciating team members' differences as key to strengthening teams and creating healthy environments.

How team leaders can navigate conflict:

> Stay neutral. Taking a side fosters feelings of betrayal and devaluing. The role of a team captain is to diffuse and offer objective thought. Similarly, your role as a team leader is to lead through objectivity while also employing empathy and understanding of why each person has behaved and feels the way they

do. Within conflict, you can pass-on this empathy and gain trust by not taking sides.

Acknowledge it. Our natural instinct is to stay out of a disagreement that does not involve us, but as a leader, this can do more harm than good. This can be seen as a dereliction of duty. As a leader, acknowledging the conflict, listening and offering paths of resolution for those in conflict enables them to take control of the outcome through collaboration.

Listen. We've mentioned a few times in this book that listening is a critical skill of a leader, and it's no less true of conflict resolution. Take the time to sit with each of the impacted parties and allow them to be heard. Use that time to clarify positions without interruption.

Stick to facts. In any conflict, there are subjective observations and facts. When meeting with each of your team members in conflict, focus on writing down the facts. This is not only important for legal purposes, but also critical in supporting paths for resolution.

Lastly, being aware of your team's needs and fostering a gateway of *communication* will motivate your team members to want to work through challenges and conflict rather than walk away from them. It's one thing to say, "my door is always open," but it is quite different to practice actively noticing challenges and opportunities among your teams when they arise. Historically, monthly team meetings or annual reviews are the opportune time to address challenges to achieving excellence—these milestone-type avenues are beneficial for setting goals and timelines for improvement. Even with monthly meetings, however, there are 9,600 minutes (at least) spent in the month on work where challenges can arise and discourage employees. That lends itself to a lot of time to pass before an employee can feel heard, and by that time, a challenge may have gone stale, or worse, the person has had time to fester on what went array. It also means more pressure and focus is on a single time frame rather than ongoing attention to and development around conflict challenges. Even in an open-door policy environment, team members may not always feel comfortable being the "squeaky wheel," so it's important for leaders to proactively seek open communication and feedback to keep teams motivated and progressing forward.

*****

A great one-on-one approach of a team captain goes beyond just looking at larger team activities and projects and understanding who your team members are individually. The characteristics of a team captain's one-on-one game are vital to not just their success as a leader but also their team's growth, ability to overcome conflict and understand one another, which creates greater success as a leader. The team captain or team leader has the unique opportunity to lead teammates through conflict and differences that otherwise could divide. To lead your team in the right direction toward victory, you must create foundational behaviors and characteristics of your team: trust, transparency, empathy, emotional intelligence, and conflict resolution. It requires intentionality, so set time aside, design exercises that build these foundations, and create avenues for accountability to ensure their consistency.

Tweetable Takeaways

Let's get social! Being able to share your growth along the way is key to transparency as a leader and building other leaders as you go. Here are important takeaways from this chapter that you can easily share on social using #LeadershipFromATeamCaptain and my handle @CiaraUngar.

- Building trust, transparency and more all happen in our one-on-one moments and cascade out into team moments.
- Distrust is contagious and if you, as the team captain, don't trust your coach or other teammates, your team will distrust you.
- Using nonverbal cues that encourage a disconnect is dangerous territory and can hurt your team's motivation.
- Be intentional about *when* and *what* you communicate to have better control over *how* you communicate - practice, create a positive environment, and use notes to keep on track.
- By maintaining a high awareness, leaders can foster safe environments that enable employees to feel comfortable enough to take calculated risks and make recommendations among their peers.
- Empathy is not the same as liking something, fixing a situation or showing sympathy.
- Empathy *is* the ability to place yourself in someone else's shoes to understand their motivations and reasoning and consider their unique perspectives.
- Empathy a verb, requiring proactive responses in order to create the greatest outcome in each situation and dynamic.

🐦 Steps to building empathy on your teams: tackle your anti-empathetic actions; offer constructive criticism in healthy ways; cultivate curiosity; solicit regular feedback from your teams.

🐦 Ways to develop empathy as a leader: step out of your comfort zone; ask for feedback; learn from others; walk a mile in someone else's shoes.

🐦 Constructive conflict can be healthy and can create fruitful outcomes of innovation and growth and bring teams closer together if navigated effectively.

🐦 Co-created solutions to conflicts are most ideal because it removes your authority and dictation from the dynamic and enables a solution that each employee can buy-into and own.

🐦 Team leaders can resolve conflicts by staying neutral; acknowledging; listening; and sticking to facts.

7

TRUST:
A PLAY-BY-PLAY

a foundation built
in every circumstance

Trust. A heavy word often discussed in personal relationship development, but more rarely addressed in professional settings. I have spent many years researching trust for personal growth and am always surprised at how squishy this topic can be when breached with others. When I think of trust, I am immediately taken back to when I was a young athlete in grade school. Among other sports, I was a cheerleader from a young age and worked hard at excelling in the sport, earning me a performance spot in the 2006 Pro-Bowl and a few college scholarships. I loved cheerleading and, to this day, embody a lot of the qualities and skills I learned from this sport (dubbing myself a bit of a Pocket Cheerleader in the office and among friends), including that of trust.

Almost more than any other sport, Cheerleading requires a high level of trust because it involves different activities like stunts, synchronization, jumps, tumbling and gymnastics where your body is at the mercy of those holding you in the air. I was a flyer, meaning I was the girl they were tossing in the air and putting on their shoulders. To make a mount successful, I had to train hard and trust my own skills to maintain control of my mechanics, weight distribution and balance. More important, I also had to trust the bases below me to properly use their skills, stay focused and in sync amidst shouting crowds and movement to keep me from falling to the ground.

As a smaller school, I cheered with the same group of girls for most of 12 years which inevitably over time created a bond. We knew each other's strengths and weaknesses well and formed friendships to varying degrees outside of games and practices, which served our team well during performances. Senior year, however, looked a bit different for our team. Toward the end of the year, I raised concerns over some chatter I heard from other seniors regarding lower classmen. This ultimately created some alienation between me and a few of the other senior members leading to what today's culture would consider mild bullying. I'm sure as adults now we would all look back on what happened and chuckle. At the time, however, it created a lot of distrust on the gym floor during games and practices. As a flyer, I relied on my teammates to hold me in the air and catch me when I fell. I relied on them to keep my head and every part of my body from hitting the ground. When relationships were strained and bullying had begun, the trust declined and our stunting undoubtedly suffered from it, increasing in falls and drops as the season came to a close.

But trust mattered in more than just cheerleading—it mattered across every sports team I was a part of. Think of the role trust plays in football and basketball—you run a play and you trust your teammate will have studied, know their position, and will show up to be your protector as you work toward scoring. Quite literally, trust is a contributing factor to success in sports and it's important for coaches and captains to understand the role that trust has within their teams and how they can develop and foster it, on and off the field.

> **Trust is an individual's belief that another individual or group of individuals will perform a particular action and the belief that that action is consistent with one's goals and objectives... A lack of trust can disrupt the team's focus, decrease performance, and contribute to the loss of a player's confidence in the team, the coach, and one another. – Jenny Nalepa[18]**

Trust is dynamic. It isn't just direct causation in one-on-one scenarios. It forms at varying levels on your teams and across your organizations across multiple scenarios—including trust in the coach, the coach's trust in the team, a teammate's trust in one another, and an individual's trust in themselves—, and it's an effect of the culture you build on your team. Being open and transparent, communicating the vision, defining roles, rewarding and encouraging consistency are just a few ways you can affect culture that directly contribute to trust-building. However, these are all very tangible ways to build trust which can often feel superficial if not balanced and authentic.

Although many of you reading this may not have been a cheer-leader, the concept of trust to avoid falling is not foreign when it comes to professional teams. If you haven't by now noticed a pattern in each chapter, building trust is a critical element to being a team captain. This is because it's the team captain's role to lead the charge in ensuring more trust and less fear is present in the workplace to avoid a toxic environment. Without this proper balance, poor performance, challenging employees, burnout, high turn-over, tensions between teams, alienation and lack of motivation or commitment will occur (all of which I've discussed throughout this book). In Fact, there's a business case for building trust. In a 2016 survey, "PwC reported 55% of CEOs believe lack of trust is a threat to their organization's growth."[19] But, a toxic environment doesn't happen simply because of bad employees that contribute to the culture; believing this to be the case can be an expensive blame game to play. Instead, those are side effects, and broken culture or toxic environment starts and ends with leadership and the trust they've built among employees.

Throughout this book, we've addressed areas of leadership that contribute to trust: consistency, interpersonal communication skills, motivation, conflict resolution, empathy, and so on. All are essential to providing a sense of safety. When your team members feel safe, they feel able to open up and take risks. When team members don't feel safe, they don't share information, they battle over responsibilities and are less likely to collaborate with one another, contributing to disappointment and inhibition from reaching their full potential. But until now, we've spoken of trust because of other behaviors, rather than trust as at the force behind our goals—it *should* be front and center in the mind of team captains and leaders every day and in every situation. Building trust is complex and occurs over time through the hundreds of moments leaders and teams have each day—not just among teams as a collective, but between leaders and their team. It forms during every play.

Becoming a trusted leader, unfortunately, does not happen by mere will. As much as I wish it were the case in both personal and professional life, you cannot will that anyone trust you inherently—it has to be earned play-by-play, moment-by-moment, consistently. In sports, behavioral predictability plays a crucial role in creating trust between coach and players, which is to say that when a coach behaves in a predictable manner, players know where they stand and have a better understanding of their coach. Consistency is critical to building trust and without it, we can't expect it from the teams we lead. In the next few sections, I'll discuss behaviors of leaders that, when maintained consistently, can begin to build a foundation of trust.

Give Trust

Trust is a two-way street. To receive trust and foster a culture of trust, you must first give trust to your team. It would not be practical nor fair to expect to receive trust and respect from others if you don't practice it yourself. Treating your staff like they're key parts of the organization or team and backing them up when challenges arise can build engagement and trust. Following the principle of behavioral predictability, a coach can trust his or her athlete to carry out a move or play because they have consistently done so in the past. Similarly, as leaders in the workplace, we should recognize where these consistencies exist, show our team members we understand the value they bring to the team, and give them more responsibility by regularly giving away authority where appropriate.

Maybe you're thinking: "What do I need to trust my team to do?" On the field, a coach has to entrust that his or her team members will listen to the plays or instructions given to them. Needing to trust your team goes beyond just being held accountable for the performance of your teams. It requires members are taking the time to develop and practice their own skills and give 100% of their effort. The same is true off the field and in the office. You can design exercises and trainings, but it only takes your team as far as they're willing to participate and grow. As a leader, trust your teams to show up in this way, just as they expect you to and create a path of accountability.

Be Open & Transparent

In my career, one of the most common hindrances to building trust and respect among teams is a lack of transparency. Unfortunately, for many leaders who don't demonstrate this quality, the workforce is increasingly demanding transparency from employers due to the digital age that allows people to learn more about their leadership and its happenings, giving employees the permission to enter leadership's personal space. In marketing, we've come to a place of realization that customers expect transparency and authenticity from brands in order to buy into them; yet, when it comes to employees, companies tend to feel there is less of this same obligation when transparency must be embraced to sustain employee retention and company growth. But the culture is quickly changing. Employees have become less accepting of inauthenticity and crave working in environments that provide them with clarity. Some companies get this really right, and some companies get this really wrong. Transparency goes beyond sharing news releases and answering questions about what their employees see in the news. At its core, being a transparent leader requires sharing information—good or bad—with your teams about current affairs and where the future of the company and their role within it may stand. It also requires that the company truly live and breathe the mantras they profess publicly.

Often, leaders struggle to see that being transparent is imperative in nearly every situation, not just little moments but the big moments, too—more important than saving face and guarding knowledge. Many managers are eager to please their teams and will make assumptions and assertions in good faith and withhold information, but then cannot fulfill what's promised putting them in an awkward situation of looking incompetent and dishonest. That's a guaranteed way to lose respect. This is because you are a human first before you are a business leader, just as your employees are humans before they are your company's means to an end. Transparency allows your teams to relate to you and, for better or worse, establishes loyalty. In being transparent with them, they'll be much more likely to have confidence in you when you can deliver on what you've said to them. Conversely, by being transparent even in the worst of times, you strengthen your leadership and influence, as people trust you as a person first, then as a leader. (Remember my story in the introduction of this book?)

Throughout my career, I have experienced an array of individuals who had inconsistent personalities and faces in the workplace depending on who the person was talking to (a common experience every professional has encountered). Inevitably, this has created the widespread notion you must always be careful who you trust in the workplace, what you say and to whom you say it. Again, we are psychologically programmed as adults to maintain our own interests firsts, whether it's to save face or keep our jobs. Although related, this notion of two-faced colleagues is quite separate from the notion of transparency from leadership and can have very different effects on your daily performance. In the beginning of this book, I walked through a scenario of an employer that has been the greatest example of lost trust I have witnessed and experienced in my career, almost solely attributed to the lack of transparency displayed. Even in the instances where we may not have all the answers, we as leadership must remain honest about our projections, expectations and decisions to avoid blindsiding our employees, which has a deeper negative impact in the long run. With that company, there has been a very high turnover rate (people leaving on their own accord), the highest I have personally witnessed and heard of firsthand. I call attention to this to showcase how a loss of trust—a loss of transparency—within an organization can directly affect your employee performance and willingness to stay, which can quickly create higher costs.

Diplomatically speaking, executive leadership intentions are not entirely to blame for a lack of transparency sometimes. Often, leadership truly believes it is being transparent because it holds monthly town halls, sends weekly company newsletters, or hosts company-wide meetings when they know announcements will be in the news. These are all valuable steps to keeping communication alive with employees, but these are not proactive or direct steps that ensure employees feel considered and have equity in the decisions made or create a culture of trust. Here is where we can turn to lessons from a team captain that display transparency.

Establish & Communicate Your Vision. As an athlete, I had several coaches and different leadership styles that I was exposed to and there is one common thread of the leaders that were most effective. The coaches that were most impactful and created the greatest loyalty were not the coaches that always gave great news or were positive motivators. The coaches that allowed themselves to be vulnerable and communicate what they knew about the team outlook gained the most trust from their players. A sense of responsibility and ownership was inadvertently passed through to each player and team captain when we felt we were part of creating and building that vision. A clear vision communicated with teams lets athletes know what direction the team is moving toward and what is expected of them, their coach and their teammates.

In business, even when agility is required, having a clearly defined vision for teams to work from as a north star allows your teams to take ownership of their role in that vision rather than chasing an ever-evolving target. Non-answers and double-talk will not get you very far because today's employee can likely see through deception even in well-intended misjudgments. Misleading or withheld communication will tarnish the trust your team has, so staying direct, honest and clear in the vision is essential in building and maintaining trust.

Give Context. Raise your hand if you've been handed a task with no context. Did you have questions that could improve the quality of your work if you had the answers? More important, how did not having context make you feel? Less important to the overall goal and outcome? Not important enough to know more information? Understanding the bigger picture is important to your team's success—not just because they can create quality work, but—because when you give information about the larger picture, it suggests that you trust your team with important information and they matter in the equation. The more visibility you provide to your teams about the present and future plans, priorities, challenges and opportunities and the thinking that went into it, the better they can stay in sync with your leadership and vision.

Show Vulnerability. As a team leader, we can often get confused on where to draw the line between keeping a team encouraged and grounded and being vulnerable when challenges or mistakes arise. Being vulnerable and exposing imperfections to your team is a key component of being transparent with your teams—it sets a precedent that transcends circumstances. If you make a mistake as a leader, admit it to your team and ask for feedback. Further, take this feedback and create positive change. Showing your vulnerability as a leader builds trust, removing the barrier between you and them and replacing it with a "we" mentality and accessible tone. When you admit your mistakes to your team, they can trust you have the ability (and bravery) to put ego aside, admit failures to contribute to the greater good of the team.

Be the Goalie. We are most familiar with the concept of a goalie, or goalkeeper, from soccer. On one level, the goalie's purpose is to keep the opposing team from scoring, but there is a lot more to this position on a team and field than meets the eye which I believe we, as leaders, can learn from. I like to think of the goalie's position more as the protector with a unique vantage point. They must pivot, maintain awareness of all the players while keeping focused on the ball. To protect their goal, they have to be great at coordinating the team and movement, instruct a change in formation, quickly redistribute the ball, and facilitate communication between players and coaches. This sounds a bit familiar, right? I see a lot of parallels between the position of a goalie and the role of a leader. Leaders are uniquely positioned on their own field to see all the moving parts of their team and guide them through pivots while maintaining awareness of how each teammate is performing and keeping focused on the ball (or the end goal of the project). It's also true that communication and facilitating good communication vertically and laterally across the field (or team) is a key component as a leader. This is an important role to fulfill every day when it comes to being a transparent leader because when you consistently show protection over your team, create lines of communication, and pivot work to best solve the challenges, you consistently earn trust.

The same role and expectations of a goalie carry through to team leadership. In this book, there are several mentions around operating from a clear and visible set of values and a vision is critical to creating team harmony and gaining trust; but, as a leader, it doesn't stop there. It's important to continuously teach and reference those values when you see teams drifting from them from your vantage point. If mistakes are made, assume the role of encouraging lessons learned from a larger viewpoint so that it's not just about the individual but rather the whole team.

Invest In and Celebrate Your Teammates

As a former cheerleader, celebrating others and being a personal "hype man" has been something I've trained for nearly my entire life. But this doesn't come naturally to many and can often be difficult to do (authentically) because it requires setting our egos and need for our own cheer squad aside, as well as requires us to keep our own positive attitude and mindfulness in check. As a leader, your teammates look to you to know and understand that you appreciate the work they put in and the job they do. It's a given. We all know feeling appreciated is important.

Remember our chapter on giving recognition? But, celebrating your team members is something that needs to be shown and demonstrated, not just stated, and instills trust on multiple levels. When you create a team culture that values each person as more than a means to an end, you improve their trust in you as well as their trust in one another. As a leader, you know your team and what they do every day better than anyone, which puts you in the unique position of getting to show how much you value your teams every single day in hundreds of ways.

First, celebrating your team members can instill confidence—in one's self, in their teammates, and in you as the team captain. As an athlete, having confidence in your coach and/or team captain means believing they are in those positions to develop your skills and invest in you. In business, feeling as though your company or leadership is invested in your success helps you to feel safe in imperfection. In both sports and business, having confidence in your leadership spills over into having confidence in yourself to make mistakes, overcome challenges, and do the job you're there to do. Sadly, despite this being a truth every professional knows on some level, the habit of celebrating our teams falls short. Summer Fridays, extra vacation days, annual Christmas parties and National Employee Appreciation Day have become crutches for many companies that have come to believe checking these boxes is enough for their employees to feel appreciated. You've employed them, you've given them a little extra money in their pocket, and you've joined in on a national holiday. While all these actions are great and are part of showing appreciation, they are not enough on their own to make your team members feel valued because there is no direct expression of how much you value them as an individual and what they contribute—an individual who spends 80% of their life ensuring you have a job the next day by keeping operations moving. It's understandable that in larger companies, executive leadership may not always be able to directly connect with each employee, even though they should try their best. Celebrating your team members at any level, however, creates a culture that is contagious across the hierarchy.

Team building and communication activities that focus on building trust, expressing gratitude, understanding and celebrating one another are great tools that enable coaches and team captains to build confidence and showcase value, but there are several steps you can take daily that don't require organized activities and have a deeper impact.

Share the Spotlight. As with any area of team leadership, encouraging your teams to share the spotlight starts with you. It's great when we as team captains can feel like we are receiving credit for the work put into developing our team, but, as mentioned earlier in this book, humility is a key characteristic of effective team captains and leaders. You'd be hard-pressed to find a team leader trusted by their team if they constantly are elbowing their way to the center of the spotlight of his or her team's successes. To earn trust, you must celebrate your team's successes collectively and individually by shining the spotlight on everyone else and stepping back into the shadows (a lesson we learned from Drew Brees). Believe it or not, when your team sees this happen, they will be motivated to want to repay you many times over.

Show Individual Appreciation. Showing your team appreciation as a team is necessary, but it should not stop there. Particularly at larger companies, showing a collective team your appreciation is simply another form in which they feel lost in the crowd and unseen. Appreciation should be shown specifically and intentionally to each of your team members. Each member of your team has their own unique strengths and weaknesses and contributes unique talent to the team's overall competency. As a team captain, identifying those unique strengths and contributions of each team member and giving them the freedom to explore new ideas and creativity and/or directly acknowledging them for having those talents will help them feel as though they matter and are important and have a direct role in the company's success. Show your appreciation by valuing another person's specific contributions and talents both verbally and nonverbally.

Be Public About it. There's an old mantra of 'praise in public, criticize in private,' and this is sadly a belief that often goes to the wayside. Too often, we rely on private emails or chats to suffice as recognition of our team members and their contributions. Praising your team members in public is without a doubt one of the most impactful steps you can take on behalf of your team to build their confidence, as well as be an ally in building their trust between executive teams. Just as showing your appreciation for team members

individually is important, singing their praises publicly as teams and as individuals is equally important. You can do this among smaller groups and across
departments, but of equal value is to get your teams
in front of the executive teams as often as possible
and in informal settings. This is a great way to build a
culture of trust between your teams and you, as well
as between your executives and your teams.

A New Generation of Leadership
Alex Morgan

At this point in your reading, we've covered many attributes and habits of a good leader as we've seen them
exemplified through team captains of all types. There's
one particular renowned athlete who has paved the way
for a new generation of leadership. Alex Morgan, a med-
alist and member of the United States Women's National
Soccer Team, is one of today's most inspirational leaders for the next generation for both her impact in society and influence on her teams. She embodies humility
and emphasizes the importance of her team members'
combined efforts to build trust, harmony and skills. In a
2016 interview, Alex talked about how there are many
ways to lead beyond just being the person giving the
pep talks at the beginning of the game. What we see
Morgan live and breathe is the ideology that being a
uniting force, valuing what each team member brings
to their wins and on the field.

Although Morgan was expected to be a leading scorer, there have been many championship games where she hasn't scored any goals. Even in those games, Morgan was doing a lot to help the team score and her leadership is just one of her roles in those wins. When senior team members like Abby Wambach retired, Morgan felt the pull into a larger leadership role, and she has carried those examples through in her career as she has stepped into the light and become a voice among young women and girls everywhere. This new role in the soccer community and on her teams is about going beyond a single win, as we see come to light when she helped champion equality in pay for women in the sports:

ABBY WAMBACH

A win for this team is a win for women everywhere," says former U.S. captain Abby Wambach. "If other women in the business world, in parenting, see these women stepping up and betting on themselves, it gives them the power to want to do it for themselves. And that, my friend, is how the world actually changes."

@CIARAUNGAR

20

At the time of this book being published, Alex Morgan has published a book that discusses leadership, and her journey in that role is just beginning. So why even mention her? Leadership isn't necessarily about trailblazing or creating an impact in the world. Sometimes leadership is more specific to your teams. Regardless of which circumstance applies to you, what can be learned from Alex Morgan is her consistency—in values, in lifting up other team members, in viewing a team as a whole unit, and in commitment to unity. In doing so, she has earned trust and respect with her teammates, coaches, and others in the industry.

Be Accountable

The last element of trust-building I'll discuss is that of accountability. Throughout this book, I touch on various ways you can show accountability and integrity, but it's worth taking a moment and reflecting on what that means as it's such a critical component of building trust with your teams. Most of the time, we believe accountability is about blaming and shaming the right employees for their mistakes. We focus on the importance of the right person owning up to mistakes they've made themselves or pointing out when others make mistakes. And although preserving credibility and holding people accountable for their actions and performance is an outcome of being accountable, it's not the whole definition.

Building trust in your organization requires the team captain to lead the way in stepping away from the idea we have to have someone to blame when something goes wrong. Mistakes are learning opportunities, and when we constantly focus on tracking mistakes, we lose the opportunity to highlight triumphs. As the team captain, you can lead the way in building trust with your teams by empowering them to also move away from a culture of blaming—holding your team leads accountable for building trust with and between their team members as a direct reflection of your vision for the team will help to build this culture organically in a grassroots manner.

Tweetable Takeaways

Let's get social! Being able to share your growth along the way is key to transparency as a leader and building other leaders as you go. Here are important takeaways from this chapter that you can easily share on social using #LeadershipFromATeamCaptain and my handle @CiaraUngar.

- It's the team captain's job to lead the charge in ensuring more trust and less fear is present in the workplace to avoid a toxic environment.
- Trust comes from consistency.
- One of the most common hindrances to building trust and respect among teams is a lack of transparency.
- By being transparent even in the worst of times, you strengthen your leadership and influence as people trust you as a person first, then as a leader.
- A loss of trust – a loss of transparency - within an organization can directly impact your employee performance and willingness to stay, which can quickly create higher costs.

- To create transparency, you can: establish and communicate your vision; give context; show vulnerability; be the goalie.

- As a leader, your teammates look to you to know and understand that you appreciate the work they put in and the job that they do.

- When you create a team culture that values each person as more than a means to an end, you improve not just their trust in you but also their trust in one another.

- Celebrating your team members can instill confidence - in one's self, in their teammates, and in you as the team captain.

- Building trust in your organization requires the team captain to lead the way in stepping away from the ideal that we have to have someone to blame when something goes from.

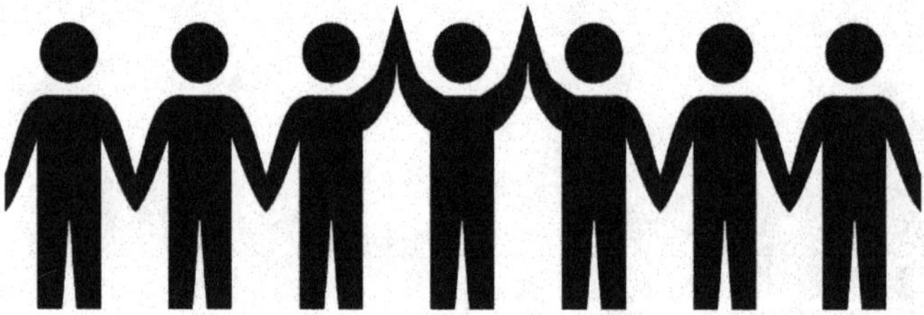

Part 3
Looking Toward Growth

8

THE GOAL LINE

I f you're finishing this book thinking all the elements we've discussed seem closely related if not repetitive at times, you're right. They're all interconnected. You can think of the qualities of a team captain and leader as all feeding into one another. Without transparency, you can't have trust. Without communication, you can't have transparency. And without one-on-one relationship building, you don't have communication. These qualities and more are markers for a great team captain, but it's not enough to simply check boxes for qualities you believe you possess as a leader. Remember, there are two levels to being a great team captain. On one level, you're building your skills: communication, subject matter expertise, organization. On another level, you're building your attributes: your mind-set, habits, behavior. These two levels complement one another from the inside out and you must practice building your intrinsic beliefs just as much as your outward skills. We must always grow and give our teams a stake in that growth—after all, their success is your success.

ACKNOWLEDGMENTS

Thank you for taking the time to read my book! I've helped many teams grow and have challenged leaders to rethink how they approach connecting with and guiding their teams. In that time, I've discovered that so many leaders feel at a loss of what to do next when seem that trying tools and training programs doesn't have the impact they want it to. Since we now live in a world with diverse team members and structures, those tools can only take us so far without fundamental principles fueling them.

I am on my own leadership journey and quest to provide other leaders in the world with new ways of thinking about their leadership styles and regain control over how they approach building teams that work well together. As a self-proclaimed Pocket Cheerleader, my goal is to help reshape your mindset so you can feel inspired and energized to lead your teams with empathy, rather than continue on with the weight of discouragement. You can find more information on leadership and emotional intelligence, including support materials for this book, at my website, CiaraUngar.com—as well as information on my other works to help you tackle individual and professional development.

I would like to take the opportunity to thank Morgan James Publishing for partnering with me in my journey to authorship. The guidance, empathy and collaboration with the Morgan James Publishing teams has been an incredible experience that I will never forget.

ABOUT THE AUTHOR

Ciara Ungar is a Certified Life & Business Coach, Consultant, Marketer and Teacher, Speaker, Author on professional and personal development, Lyme Warrior, wellness fanatic, founder of an organization that supports the homeless community, and self-proclaimed pocket cheerleader. She helps driven and motivated professionals navigate their passions, including exploring new career paths, planning for their skill growth, and building behaviors and beliefs that create empathy, mindfulness and deeper joy.

Ciara has had the opportunity to work with and for amazing brands and agencies through her marketing career, including the American Advertising Federation, Ogilvy, Sports Illustrated, AOL, PepsiCo, and more, helping them discover new ways to connect with audiences and build stronger brands. As a valued contributor to the advertising & marketing industry, she is an Innovation Women Speaker, teacher of Digital Marketing, and Forbes Contributor. She also spends considerable time devoted to bettering the community through her role as a Founder & CEO of YouAreLovd, a nonprofit organization that supports and connects the homeless community with opportunities to re-invent who they are, rebuild essential needs for self-sufficiency and socialization, and connect with a supportive community—all while spreading the message that they are loved.

Ciara earned a Bachelors in Communication, Psychology and Writing from Purdue University and a Masters from Georgetown University in PR/Corporate Communications with a focus on Integrated Marketing. She has studied and practiced in the field of psychology and communications for the last 16 years and has applied those principles to personal and professional life, challenging herself and others to show up for their own success. When Ciara was diagnosed with late stage Neurological Lyme Disease with Carditis in 2017, she found herself at a standstill as she worked through physical and cognitive rehabilitation from the damaging and lasting effects. Today, Ciara serves as an advocate for the Lyme community to bring awareness to the disease and help prevent others from experiencing damaging effects due to misinformation and lack of education. She uses this landmark moment in her life as a reminder of how delicate life is and as a motivation for pursuing her passion in personal development—using the time she has here on earth to better the world we live in.

Ciara believes that every person is unique and has something amazing to offer the world, and her purpose is to support them in recognizing their gifts and pursuing them in a way that creates fulfillment for them and inspiration to the community. She strives to have an impact that is relevant, empathetic, and unique, presenting new ways of thinking that can be applied across multiple areas of our lives.

Ciara believes in walking the talk, so she is very active in her industry, on social and in her local community in New York City, where she volunteers with New York Cares, advocacy programs, and balances work with intramural sports.

ENDNOTES

1 Cialdini, R. B., & Griskevicius, V. (2010). Social influence. In R. F. Baumeister & E. J. Finkel (Eds.), *Advanced social psychology* (pp. 385). New York, NY: Oxford University Press.

2 Gilovich, T, Keltner, D., & Nisbett, R. E. (2011). *Social psychology* (pp 276). New York, NY: W. W. Norton & Company.

3 Ballinger, L. (2018). *Understanding Socialization Efficacy and Loneliness of Baby Boomers through Facebook*. Walden University. https://scholarworks.waldenu.edu/cgi/viewcontent.cgi?article=6185&context=dissertations

4 Lauer, PhD, L., & Blue, K. (2020). *The 3 C's of Being a Captain*. Association for Applied Sport Psychology. https://appliedsportpsych.org/resources/resources-for-athletes/the-3-c-s-of-being-a-captain/

5 Lauer, PhD, L., & Blue, K. (2020). *The 3 C's of Being a Captain*. Association for Applied Sport Psychology. https://appliedsportpsych.org/resources/resources-for-athletes/the-3-c-s-of-being-a-captain/

6   Lauer, PhD, L., & Blue, K. (2020). *The 3 C's of Being a Captain*. Association for Applied Sport Psychology. https://appliedsportpsych.org/resources/resources-for-athletes/the-3-c-s-of-being-a-captain/

7   Brees, D., Brunell, M., & Fabry, C. (2010). *Coming Back Stronger: Unleashing the Hidden Power of Adversity*. Tyndale House Publishers, Inc.

8   Answers Corporation. *New Orleans Economy Still Recovering from Hurricane Katrina*. Business Answers. Accessed December 2020. http://business.answers.com/economics/new-orleans-economy-still-recovering-from-hurricane-katrina.

9   Brees, D. [drewbrees]. (2020, June 4). Black Lives Matter [Instagram Post]. Instagram. https://www.instagram.com/p/CBA1P3gHpT_/?igshid=cnn81lw8zy7

10 Welker, S. (2020, June 8). *Why Sisu, The Finnish Concept of Resilience, Might Change Your Life*. Glitter Guide. http://theglitterguide.com/2020/06/08/sisu/#:%7E:text=Sisu%20is%20a%20special%20strength,in%20reserve%20for%20hard%20times.

11 Dvorak, N., Mann, A. (2021, January 23). *Employee Recognition: Low Cost, High Impact*. Gallup. Com. https://www.gallup.com/workplace/236441/employee-recognition-low-cost-high-impact.aspx

12 Liefeld, R. (2018, April 16). *Different Doesn't Mean Wrong*. Medium. https://medium.com/@robinliefeld/different-doesnt-mean-wrong-7ba337469c2a

13 MasterClass. (2020, November 8). *Music 101: What Is Harmony and How is it used in Music?* Master Class. https://www.masterclass.com/articles/music-101-what-is-

harmony-and-how-is-it-used-in-music#how-is-harmony-represented-in-music

14 Jensen, K. (2020, November 13). *Intelligence Is Overrated: What You Really Need To Succeed*. Forbes. https://www.forbes.com/sites/keldjensen/2012/04/12/intelligence-is-overrated-what-you-really-need-to-succeed/?sh=4872b96db6d2

15 Polinamarinova1. (2020, January 27). *Silicon Valley pay tribute to Kobe Bryant the basketball legend—and investor*. Yahoo! Money | Fortune. https://money.yahoo.com/silicon-valley-pays-tribute-kobe-145456722.html

16 Kankousky, M. (2016, June 27). *9 Tips for Communicating Decisions You Don't Agree With*. Insperity. https://www.insperity.com/blog/9-tips-for-communicating-decisions-you-dont-agree-with/

17 Waal, F.,& De Waal, F. (2010). *The Age of Empathy*. Amsterdam University Press.

18 Nalepa, J. (2019, March 13). *Building Trust Within Your Team*. Michigan State University | College of Education. https://education.msu.edu/sport-coaching-leadership/uncategorized/building-trust-within-your-team/

19 Zak, P.J. (2017, February. The Neuroscience of Trust. Harvard Business Review. https://hbr-org.cdn.ampproject.org/c/s/hbr.org/amp/2017/01/the-neuroscience-of-trust

20 'You Have to Take a Stand.' Soccer Phenom Alex Morgan Wants the Respect—and—Money Female Players Deserve. (2019, May 23). TIME.com. https://time.com/magazine/us/5594338/june-3rd-2019-vol-193-no-21-u-s/

A free ebook edition is available with the purchase of this book.

To claim your free ebook edition:

1. Visit MorganJamesBOGO.com
2. Sign your name CLEARLY in the space
3. Complete the form and submit a photo of the entire copyright page
4. You or your friend can download the ebook to your preferred device

Morgan James
BOGO™

A **FREE** ebook edition is available for you or a friend with the purchase of this print book.

CLEARLY SIGN YOUR NAME ABOVE

Instructions to claim your free ebook edition:
1. Visit MorganJamesBOGO.com
2. Sign your name CLEARLY in the space above
3. Complete the form and submit a photo of this entire page
4. You or your friend can download the ebook to your preferred device

Print & Digital Together Forever.

Snap a photo

Free ebook

Read anywhere

CPSIA information can be obtained
at www.ICGtesting.com
Printed in the USA
JSHW050923190222
23123JS00001BA/18